Isaac Brock

Artist: Francine Auger

Isaac Brock, 1769-1812.

Ven Begamudré

Ven Begamudré writes realistic and speculative fiction, creative nonfiction, and poetry. His books include the novel *Van de Graaff Days* and the story collections *A Planet of Eccentrics* and *Laterna Magika* – all from Oolichan Books. He edited *Lodestone: Stories by Regina Writers* and, with Judith Krause, *Out of Place: Stories and Poems*. His upcoming books include a first collection of poems and a fantasy novel for adults and young adults. He has received the F.G. Bressani Literary Prize for Prose and the City of Regina Writing Award and has been a best book finalist in Canada and the Caribbean for the Commonwealth Writers' Prize.

Begamudré was born in South India and moved to Canada when he was six. He has also lived on the island of Mauritius. He has been writer-in-residence in the University of Calgary's Markin-Flanagan Distinguished Writers Programme, the University of Alberta's Department of English, and the Canada-Scotland Exchange. He was also the founding president of the Sage Hill Writing Experience. He has a Master of Fine Arts in creative writing from Warren Wilson College in Asheville, North Carolina.

In the same collection

Isaac Brock

Canadian Cataloguing in Publication Data

Begamudré, Ven, 1956-

    Isaac Brock: larger than life

    (The Quest Library ; 8)
    Includes bibliographical references and index.

    ISBN 0-9683601-7-3

    1. Brock, Isaac, Sir, 1769-1812. 2. Canada – History – 1791-1841. 3. Canada – History – War of 1812. 4. Lieutenant governors – Canada – Biography. 5. Soldiers – Canada – Biography. I. Title. II. Series.

FC441.B76B43 2000   971.03'2'092   C00-940655-7
F1032.B43 2000

Legal Deposit: Third quarter 2000
National Library of Canada
Bibliothèque nationale du Québec

XYZ Publishing acknowledges the support of The Quest Library project by the Canadian Studies Program and the Book Publishing Industry Development Program (BPIDP) of the Department of Canadian Heritage. The opinions expressed do not necessarily reflect the views of the Government of Canada.

The publishers further acknowledge the financial support our publishing program receives from The Canada Council for the Arts, the ministère de la Culture et des Communications du Québec, and the Société de développement des entreprises culturelles.

Chronology: Lynne Bowen
Layout: Édiscript enr.
Cover design: Zirval Design
Cover illustration: Francine Auger
Photo researcher: Marilyn Mattenley

Printed and bound in Canada

XYZ Publishing
1781 Saint Hubert Street
Montreal, Quebec H2L 3Z1
Tel: (514) 525-2170
Fax: (514) 525-7537
E-mail: xyzed@mlink.net

Distributed by: General Distribution Services
325 Humber College Boulevard
Toronto, Ontario M9W 7C3
Tel: (416) 213-1919
Fax: (416) 213-1917
E-mail: cservice@genpub.com

BROCK

Isaac

LARGER THAN LIFE

*For Andreas Schroeder,
writer-in-residence at
Regina Public Library in 1980-81.*

Contents

Preface

Although this book often reads like a novel, it's meant to be a work of nonfiction. That is to say, it's as factual as I could make it given the many challenges that anyone writing about Isaac Brock must face. Among these is the fact that, although he wrote many letters to his family and friends, he rarely wrote about his personal life.

This is why few of Brock's biographers mention his fiancée. Even those who do mention her – sometimes in a footnote – are not sure of her name or whether, indeed, she was his fiancée. I've decided that she did exist, that her name was Susan Shaw, and that they were engaged. In secret.

Some people say that a true war story is a story that's against war. I agree. I also believe that, in order to seem true, a story about a soldier is a story about the people – the men and the women – he loved. Whether Isaac Brock loved Susan Shaw is a question I've deliberately left vague. Still, as you'll see in the prologue, a true story about war is a story about our need for peace. And, as you'll see in the epilogue, a true story about death is a story about our need – every last one of us – for love.

Ven Begamudré
Regina, Canada
July 2000

A romantic death in *Battle of Queenston Heights* by J.D. Kelly. Isaac wears the star of the Order of Bath, though he died without knowing he could call himself Sir Isaac Brock, K.B.

Prologue

Brock's Last Charge

E arly on the morning of Tuesday, October 13, 1812, General Isaac Brock paused at the bottom of a hill and steadied his horse. He cursed under his breath. Leaves hissed while shuddering in the shock waves from cannon fire. Muskets crackled and spat. Shells burst in mid-air like huge falling stars that threw silhouettes among the trees – silhouettes that vanished even as they appeared.

The air felt cold and damp. He had buttoned his lapels to the throat, but he wished he had worn a stout cotton handkerchief over his cravat. Once, long ago, a similar kerchief had saved his life. But soon the sun would rise and, God willing, it would shine some warmth through the clouds that hid the stars. The real stars that should have been shining above Queenston Heights.

Behind him, a road ran westward toward a village called St. David's. Ahead of him, the Portage Road wound eastward, up the hill. Just now, though, this hill looked like a mountain.

Near the top loomed the redan battery – so called because the stone walls of this gun emplacement met in a jutting curve. The redan protected an eighteen-pound gun. Until moments ago, it had been manned by a crew of twelve British gunners. Now Americans held the battery. The British gunners huddled behind a long stone wall at the foot of the hill. About them swarmed the light company of the 49th Regiment and militia-men of the York Volunteers. Two captains were shouting at their men to take cover; to keep their eyes to the front. Still, the men kept glancing at Brock. Towering in the saddle of his horse.

The horse's name was Alfred. Tired and drenched from a long gallop, he began to shy. Brock steadied Alfred once again. Then he dismounted. He did not see who took Alfred's reins, but he could see that everyone had guessed what he was thinking. They would have to retake the battery – even if this meant charging up the hill. Even if it meant charging straight into enemy fire. Yet he knew these men, especially the soldiers of the 49th Foot. Some of them had served with him for over ten years, on both sides of the Atlantic, and he knew. They would follow him anywhere.

What Brock did not know was who had captured the redan battery – except that they were Americans.

They were, in fact, men from the Sixth, Thirteenth, and Twenty-Third Regiments, led for the moment by a Captain John Wool. At twenty-four, he was almost nineteen years younger than Brock and equally daring. Wool had led these men along a fisherman's path that climbed from the bank of the Niagara River all the way up the gorge to Queenston Heights. He had done this in the dark. After the men had reached a wood between the gorge and the summit of the hill, he had spread them among the trees to provide covering fire while other men had stumbled up the path. Then Wool had frowned. All the huts – those overlooking the river on one side, those overlooking the hill road on the other – had seemed empty. Even more odd, the battery itself had been lightly guarded. With sixty officers and men, Wool had attacked. A dozen gunners had fled downhill, but not before they had spiked the gun.

Now Wool cursed under his breath, and not for the first time since having captured the redan. He cursed because he could not turn the gun on the British so that other Americans, pinned to the river-bank by cannon and musket fire, could move forward. He cursed because he was in pain.

He was leaning against the curving stone wall of the redan. He could not sit down because, an hour earlier, he had been wounded in the buttocks. Of all the shameful, ridiculous things. But if he held this battery while the rest of the American force crossed the river, no one would remember him for his wound. They would remember him as the daring young captain who had turned the tide of battle well before sunrise. He looked down and groaned. If he so much as moved, his feet squelched in his shoes. They were filling with the blood that ran down the backs of his legs.

At the bottom of the hill, Brock climbed over the long stone wall. With his left hand, he straightened his lapels. He had known the ride would be wet, and so, instead of pulling on his major-general's coat, he had pulled on an older coat he had worn as a brigadier. Now it was splattered with mud. So were his breeches. So were his high, tasselled boots.

He straightened his cocked hat and drew his sword. Then, with regulars and militiamen hard on his heels, he ran up the hill. The ground was slippery with fallen leaves, but he still ran – into the teeth of enemy fire. He felt young again, no longer forty-three. Although he was as fit as many younger men, one by one they began overtaking him. One by one, they began to fall. Here a man clutched his stomach. There a boy clutched his thigh. Scarlet figures, men and boys, staggered before coming to rest – some doubled in pain, others with an arm outflung. All of them so young.

No one, least of all Brock, was sure what happened next. Not even the Americans were sure, though one of them claimed he knew exactly what had happened. He knew, he said, because he did it.

His name was Robert Walcot, he was in the Thirteenth Regiment, and he had been ordered to stay with the captured gun. He called himself an artillerist. He was also a good shot with a musket, and when he heard his fellow Americans open fire, he crept forward to look. Red coats glowed in the grey morning light. The British and Canadians had gone mad. No staying among the trees, no taking cover. They were charging straight up the steep hill. Walcot shouted to a friend to hand him a musket. He loaded it with extra shot and took aim. With all the figures charging toward him, he had his choice of targets. He took his time because he was looking for an officer. There was more than one, so he aimed at the tallest officer in sight. This one wore a cocked hat. His scarlet coat, though spattered with mud, bore gold epaulettes. Musket fire glinted off his sword.

Walcot squeezed the trigger.

Still running uphill, Brock turned to urge his men onward. He turned to shout, "Forward, the 49th! Push on, the York Volunteers!" But, moving as one, two musket balls punched through his chest, just above his heart. They tore through his body and out his left side. The side on which he fell.

Looking up, he saw a young man – a boy, really – run to him and fall to his knees. The boy shouted, "Are you much hurt, sir?"

Brock could not reply. He was trying to recall the boy's name. Jarvis? Jervis? A Canadian volunteer in the 49th. He was fifteen. Brock knew this because once, during an inspection, he had asked the boy how old he was. Then Brock had said that he, too, had been fifteen when he had entered the King's service. The boy's eyes had shifted to the epaulettes, and Brock had read his mind. One day, Jarvis or Jervis had been thinking, he might wear gold braid and a cocked hat. He, too, might be a general.

At last, Brock moved his left hand to his breast. With his right hand, he tried to find his sword yet clutched up only fallen leaves. Red maple leaves. Oak leaves beginning to yellow. They were all damp. His left side was also damp. His eyes refused to stay open. If only the clouds would part. All about him were smells. The heavy, pungent smell – still on his clothes and skin – of Alfred's drenched coat. The acrid smell of gunpowder. The boy's tears, which smelled like the sea.

Then came other smells, other sounds, other sights. The salt of the North Sea, the laughter of boys and girls, the granite cliffs of Guernsey. Wind rustling through palm trees in Barbados. Or was it Jamaica? Sand hills dissolving in a rain beating down on windmills. Ice. The yardarms and rigging of a ship of the line coated with ice. A pale man with one arm. The smell of melting red wax. A midnight boat chase across a lake. Had there been a moon? He could not remember. How odd that a soldier should have spent most of his life near water. Beeswax candles. Jewels and silk. Rivers, lakes, trees, mud. Always mud. Always rain and snow and ice.

When Brock started shivering, he opened his eyes. He could still hear cannon fire and musket fire, but the sounds were muted now. Then the sun burst through the clouds. Two suns. How could this be? Fireflies, then. No, not even that. Floating high above him were the radiant faces of two women. The older woman was smiling. The younger woman wept. He knew who they were. How could he not know? They were the only two women he had ever loved.

And then he knew that the end was near. And then, he knew.

1

Young Master Isaac

Isaac Brock was born on Friday, October 6, 1769 in St. Peter Port on Guernsey, one of the Channel Islands. These islands belong to Britain but are close to France and, at one time, were part of the Duchy of Normandy. South of the islands is the Gulf of St. Malo. In the mid-sixteenth century, Jacques Cartier sailed from the port of St. Malo – first, to Newfoundland and the Gulf of St. Lawrence; later, up the St. Lawrence River to an Iroquois village called Hochelaga, which became the city of Montreal.

But Master Isaac, as friends and family called him, cared little about North America because life in Guernsey depended more on events in England and

Isaac's Aunt Susan guessed only half right: her brother, James, would become not only an admiral but also Lord de Saumarez.

France than on events across the Atlantic. At the same time, the people of Guernsey, like the people of Jersey and of other Channel Islands, were fiercely independent. True, they owed their allegiance to the British Crown; yet they managed many of their own affairs and, on official occasions, they spoke French. At home, Isaac spoke English, but when he played with friends he spoke like them in patois – a regional dialect that varied from island to island. Even the cattle varied from island to island. Guernsey had its brown and white Guernsey cows; Jersey had its fawn-coloured Jersey cows. These largest of the Channel Islands were good-natured rivals, and Isaac would not have been in school very long before he heard this old joke:

"Why is every good Guernseyman glad to see a red sky at night?"

"Hmm," Isaac might have replied. "Red sky at night, sailor's delight?"

"Non, Master Isaac. Because the Guernseyman thinks that Jersey is on fire!"

Isaac attended Elizabeth College. It had been founded by Good Queen Bess – Queen Elizabeth I – some two decades before her fleet, led by Sir Francis Drake, had defeated the Spanish Armada in 1588. At twelve pounds a year, the tuition was reasonable. Isaac's masters taught a range of subjects: classical languages like Latin and Greek; modern ones like Italian and French; fencing and drilling, both of which he liked; and drawing and music, both of which he pretended he disliked. Though, at home, he enjoyed himself when his sisters taught him to dance. He was not the most conscientious of pupils – as his headmaster,

Reverend Crispin, often pointed out. No, Isaac preferred games to studies. He became a good boxer and a strong swimmer. When he was not playing with friends, he explored the countryside and shore near St. Peter Port. The town lay at the end of a narrow valley between high cliffs. Clutching wiry gorse, he climbed to the cliffs, then walked along the edge. After a while, he flopped among the heather. He looked out to sea or up at the sky and here he saw clouds shaped like castles or knights. There had been castles and knights in his family's past, as his father never tired of reminding him. And even if Isaac grew easily bored at school, he never tired of hearing his father's tales. Often the same tale, again and again.

One of Isaac's ancestors on his father's side had been Sir Hugh Brock, a follower of the English King Edward III. Sir Hugh was said to be a tenacious warrior – as befitted his family name, for in Old English, Brock meant badger. Brock could also mean a foul, dirty fellow, but Isaac's father reminded his sons that they were neither foul nor dirty. They were gentlemen. The Brocks of Guernsey even had their own coat of arms, with a lion and a gold fleur-de-lis below a scallop shell. And Sir Hugh? He was as valiant as he was said to be stout. Late in the fourteenth century, he was keeper of the Castle of Derval, in Brittany, when this northwest corner of France was a duchy of England. But, during the Hundred Years' War, the French forced the English out of Brittany. It was said that Sir Hugh chose Guernsey as his family's new home. The island was far enough from France for an English knight to feel safe yet close enough for him to see the lands that he and his ailing king had lost.

This was all Isaac's father remembered about the distant past. He did not need to remind the children of his own immediate ancestors, but this did not stop him.

Isaac's paternal grandfather, William Brock, was a gentleman who had died three years before Isaac had been born. William's three sons and daughter had all married well. The eldest son, also called William, had married Judith de Beauvoir. She hailed from a proud and wealthy Guernsey family, and it seemed to Isaac that his Aunt Judith was far too proud of their wealth. The youngest son, Isaac's Uncle Henry, had married Susan Saumarez, whose brother James – he was twelve years older than Isaac – was earning accolades in the Royal Navy. Aunt Susan predicted that her brother would one day become an admiral. At family gatherings, she looked about as though expecting someone to contradict her. No one did. The few times Isaac had seen his Uncle James home on leave, Isaac had promised himself that he, too, would earn accolades in the Royal Navy. But he told no one of this dream. As for William's only daughter, Isaac's Aunt Mary, she had married a gentleman named John Le Marchant.

Then there was William's second son, Isaac's father John. In his youth he had been a midshipman in the Royal Navy and sailed as far away as India. According to him, he had made the best marriage of all. Hearing this, Isaac's mother would scoff. John would laugh, Isaac's sisters would giggle, and Isaac and his brothers would not know what to make of their mother's response.

Not to be outdone by her husband, Elizabeth Brock also tried to tell the children about her ancestors. But with all the housework to be done – even with the help of two daughters – she rarely had time for spinning tales. She had been born a De Lisle. Her mother, Rebecca, had been born a Carey. One of Elizabeth's ancestors, Sir John De Lisle, had been governor of Guernsey in the early fifteenth century, during the reign of the English King Henry IV. And her father, Isaac's maternal grandfather, had been lieutenant bailiff of Guernsey when she married John. How could she know that Isaac would one day follow in her father's footsteps? Not on Guernsey but on the other side of the Atlantic, in a colony called Upper Canada.

For that matter, how could Isaac know what the future would hold? All he saw in the sky was his family's glorious past. Feeling quite satisfied with himself, he looked more closely at the clouds. They looked like sailing ships now, and he grinned. Then, seeing that the sun was dropping beyond the far side of the island – to set in the English Channel, which led to the North Atlantic – he made his way home.

Home was a fine house of blue-grey granite in the centre of St. Peter Port. John Brock had bought this house eleven years after marrying Elizabeth. They had taken possession of it on Michaelmas, toward the end of September, and Isaac had been born seven days later. Elizabeth often told him there was a bond between him and this house. He wanted to ask whether this meant he should never leave St. Peter Port, but he already knew that he must – to sail to the Mediterranean or as far away as India. By then, perhaps, his Uncle James truly would be an admiral, with his own flag, and Isaac would be his flag captain. True, he would have to begin as a midshipman, but surely a boy who claimed descent from Brocks and De Lisles – with their ties to families named Saumarez, de Beauvoir, Le Marchant – would not remain a midshipman for long?

∽

On a June day in the summer before Isaac turned ten, he stood panting from his run to the Tour Beauregard and looked east. This tower had been built on the main shore of St. Peter Port to protect the roadstead, the sheltered offshore anchorage for ships. There were many ships. Some were merchantmen that brought wine to Guernsey from Gascony, in the southwest corner of France. Others were privateers. Unlike piracy, privateering was respectable because a privateer sailed under letters of marque from the king – to whom the privateer owed a share of his profits. As far as Isaac knew, no one in his family had been a privateer, but it seemed like an exciting life, and he craved excitement.

This was one reason he was looking at Castle Cornet.

The castle stood on the northern end of a small tidal islet 800 metres away. He had been there many times, always by boat because tides here could rise as high as twelve metres. The castle's present form was largely due to rebuilding in the time of Good Queen Bess, and her coat of arms appeared over the gate in the town bastion. Even if Isaac was not the best of students at Elizabeth College, he knew all the stories about the castle. His favourite was about the great explosion of 1672. One night in late December, lightning had struck the keep and the magazine. The explosion had killed the governor's wife and his mother, but the incident had had a darkly humorous twist – for the explosion had blown the governor, still in his bed, onto the battlements. After the explosion the castle had been rebuilt, not for the first time, and not as a palace but a fortress.

There was another reason Isaac was looking at the castle: he did not want to think about his father. Before Isaac had run to the Tour Beauregard, he had been with his family at the parish church of St. Peter. There the Brocks and De Lisles, de Beauvoirs and Le Marchants had attended a special service marking the anniversary of a death. The death of Isaac's father.

Two summers before, in June of 1777, John Brock had gone to Dinan, in Brittany, to take the healing waters. He had gone with his third son, Daniel, who had then been fourteen. And there, in the land that had once belonged to England – the land Sir Hugh Brock had fled – John had died. He had been only forty-eight and Isaac not yet eight. He had known his father was ill but had not realized how ill. John had left Elizabeth a widow. He had left their ten children fatherless. There should have been fourteen, but four of them – two boys, two girls – had died early on. No one in the family spoke of them. And if Isaac resented being the third youngest of eight sons, he never said so. He had other ways of proving he was just as good as his five elder brothers.

Ready at last, he walked to the water's edge, stripped off all his clothes except his breeches, and dove into the harbour.

He shuddered but refused to gasp. He surfaced and, with bold strokes, made for Castle Cornet. How hard could it be, he thought, to swim half a mile? But he had forgotten the strong tides that ran between the quay and the islet. Still, it was a fine day, with no sign of the southwesterly gales that could blow up with little warning. And so he swam.

He swam strongly, furiously, as though he could bring his father back to life; bring laughter back to the fine granite house in the middle of St. Peter Port. There, even now, the family was gathering for a meal, but Isaac was not hungry. Aunt Judith had insisted on providing it all. Knowing her, the food would be sumptuous. Not for her the simple dishes John had once enjoyed, especially lobster. Why, only last week, she had sent her cook to teach Elizabeth how to make a special loin of lamb – roasted with a pitu crust of garlic, basil, and Parmesan.

Isaac's stomach felt empty now. It was like an air-filled bladder that kept him afloat. Good thing, too. His hunger would help him swim, help him reach the castle. It looked farther away than it had from the shore. Much farther.

Half way to the islet, he stopped to rest. He treaded water and eyed Castle Cornet as though it was held by the enemy. Early in the Hundred Years' War, the French had captured the castle and built up its battlements and the round keep. A clever enemy, though. They had mixed seashells into the mortar to give it strength. Yes, the French had always been the enemy, and there his father had gone and died in France.

Waves lapped at Isaac's face. When he carelessly inhaled, water filled his nose, then ran down his throat. He coughed the water out. Salt grated on his tongue; salt tickled the roof of his mouth. But he was fine. A moment's rest, and he could go on. If only his brothers could see him – especially his first two brothers, but they were far away. John, the eldest at twenty, was a lieutenant with the 8th Regiment, the King's Regiment. Ferdinand, the second eldest at nineteen, was with the 60th Regiment, the Royal Americans. Both were on the far side of the Atlantic. Isaac had not seen them in years.

Still treading water, he moved his arms and legs and tried to remain afloat. He was tiring now. At any moment, he would sink. What had he been thinking of? Then again, it was not winter or spring or autumn. In those seasons, he would never have attempted the swim. He would have lasted five minutes at most in these cold waters of the North Sea. Five minutes before his limbs froze and he sank to a numbing death. But it was early summer now, it was June, it was two years since his father had died, and Isaac would not turn back.

From off to the right, he saw a lugger approach and heard its master call out. The man asked whether Isaac needed help. Instead of shaking his head, he kicked his legs to bring his body almost parallel to the surface. He swam once more. He did not know where the strength came from but, slowly, surely, he covered the remaining 400 metres to the islet. He pulled himself out of the water and sat on a rock. At once, he began to shiver, and so he slipped back into the water. He eyed the white buildings of the town; he looked at the flanking cliffs; and, once more, he began to swim. An hour later, shivering in his wet clothes, dripping water onto the floor of his house, he stood in the parlour doorway and looked at a familiar gathering: Uncle William with Aunt Judith de Beauvoir; Uncle Henry with Aunt Susan Saumarez; Aunt Mary with Uncle John Le Marchant; Isaac's five brothers who still lived at home; and their two lovely sisters. Then he looked at his mother, Elizabeth, who was adding sugar to her tea. He felt triumphant in a way he could not explain. He refused to flinch when she cried, "Isaac Brock, what have you done!"

He also refused to answer her. He had done what no other boy his age could do, and he would keep it to himself till he could do it without having to rest half way. Still, could she not guess? Could none of them – with their cups of tea, their glasses of punch – guess what he had done? His father would have guessed. He would have understood. And, oh, how proud he would have been.

Perhaps the only portrait, this one by J. Hudson, showing Isaac full face. Like his biographers, most painters based their depictions of Isaac on historical evidence and hearsay.

2

A Sword, a Fever, a Duel

Thirty-two years later, in the autumn of 1811, a young woman named Susan Shaw asked Isaac a simple question to which he had no simple answer. He had recently turned forty-two. They were engaged, and though they spent much time together when he was not dashing about the Canadas, he did not want to announce their engagement. She reluctantly agreed. In return she held him to certain promises – such as answering questions about himself. He, too, agreed, though he had no intention of answering all of them in detail. And he could not reveal that his family was facing financial ruin. Her question now was this: why, if he had been so fascinated by the sea as a boy, had he become a soldier?

They were strolling on a lawn behind a small, wood frame legislative building. This was one of the few patches of lawn in the muddy town of York, the capital of Upper Canada. One day, Upper Canada would be called Ontario, and York, no longer quite so small or muddy, would be called Toronto.

The afternoon was warm for late October, and though Isaac would be meeting soon with certain important legislators, he seemed unwilling to rush the stroll. Susan hoped that the question she had posed would lead to a long answer. It did. She congratulated herself on distracting him, at least for a while, from his endless affairs of state.

Isaac supposed there had been two reasons he had joined the army – one practical, the other frivolous. Looking back, it seemed to him that the frivolous reason had been far more important than the practical one. As is often the case with young men, Susan added. Then she kept quiet, and the longer he rambled, the more she felt she knew him. If it were possible for any young woman to know a man who guarded his private life so well.

Even as Isaac finished his education at the age of fifteen, his eldest brother, John, bought his own commission as a captain in the 8th Regiment. The King's Regiment. True, their Uncle James Saumarez was blazing a path through the naval officers' lists and so could easily help Isaac's career, but Elizabeth felt he would be happier – and safer – if John could keep an eye on him. He was home after having spent ten years in America. As for Isaac's second eldest brother, Ferdinand – a lieutenant in the 60th Regiment, the

Royal Americans – he had died at the Battle of Baton Rouge. He had been nineteen.

On June 21, 1779, Spain had declared war on Britain. Spain had done this not only to help the Thirteen Colonies in their revolt against the British Crown but also to conquer British lands along the Mississippi. Trust Spain to further her own interests, John said. Ferdinand died three months later, on September 21, two weeks before Isaac's tenth birthday – but the news did not reach Guernsey till late November.

Isaac came home from his new school – in England, in Southampton – to observe a sad Christmas. It was a bitter one, as well. For, although Ferdinand had been killed by Spanish cannon fire, Elizabeth despised the Americans and their revolt. Colonial upstarts, she called them. Filthy, rebellious rabble. And so Isaac, who loved his mother almost as much as he had loved his father, decided that Britain no longer had a single mortal enemy. She had two: France, as always; and, from now on, the United States of America.

Five years later, when he joined the King's Regiment, he asked John whether Ferdinand might have lived had he also joined the 8th instead of the 60th. John told Isaac not to be a fool. True, brothers could look out for one another, but no one was impervious in war. Not even a Brock.

Even as Isaac finished saying this, he glanced at Susan. She was nodding in agreement. She was, after all, a general's daughter. Then she asked him the frivolous reason he had joined the army: the one a young man would find far more important.

Why, he exclaimed. Could she not guess? He had liked the uniform.

One of Isaac's six remaining brothers – Savery, the second youngest – was a midshipman in the Royal Navy. He was proud of his white shirt and trousers, his coat with silver buttons, his top hat and his dirk. But Isaac admitted that he found the navy blue coat much plainer than John's scarlet one. And John bore no mere dirk but a sword. At this, Savery reminded Isaac that British soldiers were called lobsterbacks. Better a lobsterback than a frog, Isaac retorted. So it was that, when he was fifteen and a half, he bought his first commission – for 400 pounds – and donned the uniform of an ensign in His Britannic Majesty's Army.

What a uniform it was, ordered by Elizabeth from the best tailor in St. Peter Port. While John helped Isaac dress upstairs, she waited in the parlour with his aunts: Judith de Beauvoir, Susan Saumarez, and Mary Le Marchant.

Isaac's white waistcoat and breeches fit him like gloves. So did the black gaiters rising to his knees. Around his waist, John tied a crimson sash with its tassels dangling just so. After fussing with Isaac's cravat, John tied a gilt gorget in place with blue silk ribbons. The gorget, shaped like a crescent and etched with the royal arms, was a relic from earlier times of the armour that had protected a knight's throat.

"Sir Isaac Brock," John quipped. Then he helped Isaac into his coat and brushed lint off its facings.

Like the background of the regimental colours carried into battle, the facings of the 8th Regiment were blue – as were the facings of all regiments called

King's or Queen's. These facings picked out the lapels of the scarlet coat; its wide cuffs; and the two false pocket flaps on the swallow-tailed back. The white officers' lace of the 8th Regiment was interwoven with gold. Gold lace also trimmed the hat with its black cockade, and the epaulette on Isaac's right shoulder. His hat was in its box.

Over the coat, John strapped a white belt that crossed from the epaulette down toward Isaac's left hip. The oval plate at the breast bore the regimental badge, a silver horse in a crowned garter. Last came the sword, a gift from all three aunts. Called a spadroon, it had a straight blade and stirrup hilt. Around the grip, which was made of bone, a locket bore the badge: the horse in the garter. And, ignoring the practice of the 8th Regiment, the aunts had insisted that the fittings of the sword and its scabbard should be gold.

Isaac shook his head now while describing the tears in his mother's eyes when he had entered the parlour. He laughed heartily, and Susan glanced away while he wiped his own eyes.

He used a handkerchief. It had been embroidered with his monogram by a certain lady during his days as a brigadier, but Susan told herself that she did not mind. She was embroidering a new set of handkerchiefs with a lion, a fleur-de-lis, and a scallop shell; with his family's coat of arms. Smiling over how pleased he would be with her gift, she dreamt that one day she would play all four roles: Elizabeth's and the aunts'. One day, she, Mrs. Isaac Brock, would wait in her parlour each time one of her sons donned his first uniform and his dazzling new sword. No, not Mrs. Brock. Their father – no longer merely a major-general, as he was now – would be a Knight of the Bath. Perhaps even a peer: Viscount Brock. And Susan, the envy of her sisters, would be Viscountess Brock.

∞

Without further prompting, Isaac continued the story of his early years in the army. First, though, he glanced at the back door of the small legislative building. He had asked one of his officers to tell him when the legislators arrived, and Susan was glad to see that no one stood in the doorway. She allowed Isaac to lead her back the way they had come.

· He raised his cocked hat to gentlemen who nodded while they passed. Like her, he was grateful that no one stopped to chat. There were times a man deserved to be left alone, especially if he had just been made president and administrator of the government of Upper Canada. And if he was with the lovely Miss Shaw. Whenever she teased him by saying that most high officials were pompous bores, he secretly flattered himself that he was not just another high official. Then again, he did wonder whether his successes had been due to skill or to plain, blind luck.

He glossed over his early years in uniform. After the disasters of the American Revolution, these were welcome years of peace. He spent much of his time alone with books, which he should have done while in school. He also continued to fence and box and swim. And to improve his horsemanship. He did not rise as quickly as he had hoped, but Elizabeth was happy because peacetime kept him either in Guernsey or Jersey or in nearby England. But the more she reminded him of his bond with the fine granite house, the more he craved excitement. After six years of chafing as an ensign, he rose at last to lieutenant.

The following year, at twenty-two, he was gazetted – his name officially published – as a captain. Without consulting John, Isaac changed regiments. To the 49th Foot. Its officers' lace was gold like the lace of the 8th Regiment, but the facings of the 49th, like the background of its regimental colours, were a type of green called full green.

He changed regiments so that he could be posted abroad, and Elizabeth worried for him because the 49th was stationed in the West Indies. This was a hazardous place because, for every man who died in battle there, ten men died of disease. As did Isaac's cousin, Henry Brock, a lieutenant in the 13th Foot. As Isaac nearly did.

This was during his second year in the West Indies, he told Susan – the year he spent in the town of Kingston on the island of Jamaica. During his first year, on Barbados, he had engaged a servant named Dobson who did everything from caring for uniforms to searching out certain kinds of wine. And, in Jamaica, nursing Isaac through yellow fever. Dobson returned with him to Guernsey, where Isaac finished recovering; where he once more went for long walks along the cliffs. Though he no longer dreamt of castles and knights. After this, Dobson followed him to the recruiting service in England and life became dull again. But Elizabeth was glad to have Isaac back.

He was grateful now that Susan seemed to be thinking of Elizabeth; that Susan did not press him for details about the fever. There were certain things a gentleman could not tell a lady. It would be another century before doctors would understand that yellow fever was transmitted by mosquitoes. Until then, such diseases would continue inciting horror: the horror Isaac felt even now, twenty years after he had recovered. Horror because, while the British may have given the disease a seemingly innocent name, the locals used a more vivid one. In Spanish they called it *vomito negro*. Black vomit.

First came the fever, so intense that even a man as strong as Isaac could not get out of bed. Then the victim's kidneys failed him, though by now he was so ill that he did not know this. He could not stop vomiting. His skin turned yellow from jaundice and itched as though a thousand tiny insects were crawling under the skin. Dobson would hold Isaac's hands on either side of his pillow to keep him from scratching till he bled. So Dobson told Isaac, months after he recovered.

Henry Brock was less fortunate. Thankfully, his end was as swift as it was horrible. He began bleeding inside, bleeding so much that he vomited blood. And the pain of it – as though, with each spasm, he would spew out his guts till he turned himself inside out. Then he became delirious and shouted till he lost his voice. Then he fell unconscious. At last he slipped quickly and quietly into death.

Isaac shook his head now. He had craved excitement and found it under blue tropical skies. Excitement of a sort. For, when yellow fever struck, as it did every few years in the West Indies, three out of four men died. Isaac had been among the one in four who had lived. Thanks to Dobson. Thanks to fate.

∞

Before Isaac and Susan turned at the end of the strip of lawn, they paused. He watched her frown at the greying sky as though wondering whether it might snow. Then she turned with him and they strolled once again. The pale shadows of afternoon were lengthening. Perhaps because the air was growing chill, she wanted to hear more about the West Indies. Her father had hinted once that Isaac had survived a duel there. Then her father had teased her by saying that Isaac had won the duel without firing a shot. When she asked him about it now, he laughed. A man and wife who passed them smiled. Susan nodded her greeting, and Isaac raised his cocked hat, but they did not stop. They quickened their step for warmth, and he told her of his one and only duel.

This was during his first year in the West Indies, his year on Barbados, one of the Windward Isles. When he arrived in 1791, soldiers were still telling tales of the hurricane of eleven years before. It had been the worst in memory. Passing through the Caribbean Sea in October of 1780, the hurricane had destroyed merchant fleets, two naval fleets – one British, one French – and killed 22,000 men, women, and children. The wind had been so fierce that the rain had stripped the bark off trees.

But Isaac's year in Barbados held no such excitement. Life for soldiers here was dull. Their regiments were in the West Indies, as were naval squadrons, to guard the major trading routes for sugar and tobacco. Months went by with nothing to do but drill, which the soldiers did on a parade ground called the Savannah, outside Bridgetown on the island's southwest coast. And there was little for officers to do but explore the island – to race on horseback up Mount Hillaby or watch African slaves working sugar cane fields – and to quarrel.

There was a captain in the 49th, an Englishman Isaac now refused to name, who enjoyed tormenting junior officers. He was a crack shot with a pistol and had never lost a duel. One day, he began taunting Isaac about a Guernseyman's being good for nothing but tending gardens and smuggling brandy.

Isaac tried to ignore these taunts, but they reminded him of his four years of school in Southampton. Dreary Southampton. The tides there rose only centimetres, not twelve metres as they did in St. Peter Port. What kind of tide rose the length of a finger? A feeble, English tide. Even the bullying of the English schoolboys had been feeble, and so he had taught them how to box. Taught them till their eyes blackened and their noses bled. This was why, when the captain began insulting Isaac's mother and sisters, he could bear it no longer, and so he demanded satisfaction. Gladly, the captain said. His eyes brightened at the prospect of giving yet another greenhorn a fatal lesson in marksmanship.

Alone in his room that night, Isaac cursed the blood that made Brocks so tall. At twenty-two, he had reached his full height. He stood nearly 190 centimetres in his stocking feet – six feet, two inches – when most men stood perhaps 165 centimetres – five feet, five inches. Men like the captain. This could make all the difference in a duel because, at the regulation twelve paces, the taller man made such a good target. And here the shorter man was also a crack shot. Isaac's face broke into sweat. After reaching under his pillow, he took out a handkerchief – one of the large cotton handkerchiefs that his mother had embroidered for him. He soaked it in water that Dobson had left beside the bed, wrung out the water and, meaning to wrap the handkerchief around his brow, pulled it to its full length of forty-five centimetres. Barely a single pace.

This was when he began to laugh. He laughed so loudly that he woke Dobson, who rushed in to ask what was wrong. Nothing, Isaac replied. He continued to laugh while Dobson, shaking his head, left. After this Isaac could not sleep – but it was excitement, not worry, that kept him awake till dawn.

He and the captain met on a secluded beach of white sand. Trade winds rustled in the fronds of coconut palms. Waves rolled across the coral reefs offshore. The two men wore their white breeches and waistcoats but not the scarlet coats whose sleeves impeded movement. Isaac's eyes were bloodshot from lack of sleep. The captain saw this and smiled. Their seconds loaded two pistols and checked that the flintlocks were secure. Then the seconds handed the pistols to the principals and stood to one side. But when the captain turned to measure out his six paces, Isaac called for the captain to face him once more.

"You will agree," Isaac said, "that as the injured party I may set the terms of the duel?"

The captain nodded warily while the seconds frowned.

"And," Isaac said, "given the difference in our heights, would you not agree that we should duel on equal terms? Especially as you, sir, are the better shot."

The captain sighed. At last he nodded in agreement.

"Well, then," Isaac said. He removed a clean handkerchief he had tucked into the crimson sash tied around his waist. Holding the handkerchief by one corner, he asked the captain to hold the opposite corner.

The captain did this, all the while looking at Isaac as if he had gone mad. The seconds appeared to think so, too. They stared with disbelief while Isaac pressed the muzzle of his pistol into the captain's brow. At last Isaac said, calmly:

"Say the word, my good sir, and we shall fire, both as one. Not over a distance of twelve paces but across the length of this kerchief, whose embroidery you would no doubt call unrefined."

The captain was a bully but not a fool. He would die as surely as Isaac would. If the captain had to become a laughingstock, better that he should live than die. He refused to proceed, and the seconds took note. By nightfall, the story had made the rounds of the barracks fronting the Savannah, and the captain found himself laughed out of the regiment. He bought passage on a merchant ship bound for England and was never heard from again. As for Isaac, soon all the 4,000 officers and men stationed in Barbados knew him by sight. He was one of the Guernsey Brocks. Tall, strapping fellow. Brilliant strategist, utterly mad.

Not that Isaac said these last to Susan. He had expected her to laugh but she only chuckled while shaking her head. Then, seeing one of his officers in a doorway of the legislative building, she stopped and raised a gloved hand to him.

He bowed with mock formality. His name was John Macdonell; he was twenty-four and a lieutenant-colonel. He was also the acting attorney general of Upper Canada. She knew him well because he was engaged to her friend, Mary Powell, the youngest daughter of Justice William Dummer Powell. How splendid a double wedding might be, Susan thought – the brides in white, the grooms in scarlet and gold. Mary thought so, too, as did John. Susan had not yet told Isaac because she did not want to annoy him. She smiled to herself. With all his cares, his military and civil affairs of state, would he even find the time to attend his own wedding? Knowing him, he would send an aide-de-camp in his place.

She realized that Isaac was steering her toward her carriage. After she climbed into it, she gestured for him to stay a moment longer. He did, though Macdonell was looking impatient. At last she asked what had happened to Isaac's eldest brother. Ferdinand had died at Baton Rouge, but where was John? Isaac looked taken aback and she cursed her curiosity. Then he said that John had exchanged the blue facings and gold lace of the 8th Regiment for the buff facings and silver lace of a newer regiment, the 81st. He had still been their commander when he had died ten years ago, in July of 1801, at the Cape of Good Hope. He had been forty-two, the same age Isaac was now.

Susan said she was sorry. When Isaac said it no longer bothered him, she asked her last question. For now. Had John been mortally wounded in battle or had he been felled by some dreaded South African disease?

"Neither," Isaac said, stepping away from the carriage. "John was killed in a duel."

3

A Truly Charmed Life

In May of 1844, almost thirty-two years after the Battle of Queenston Heights, Ferdinand Brock Tupper returned to Guernsey from his travels in South America. His mother, Elizabeth Brock Tupper, gave him sad news: her only surviving brother, Savery, was losing his mind. He was not mad. He was simply old, although at seventy-one, he was eight years younger than she was; and, as Ferdinand should note, she was very much in her mind.

Thirty years ago, she said, an officer who had served with the 49th Foot had sent Savery a box of letters and some trunks. They had belonged to Ferdinand's Uncle Isaac. Savery had never opened

THE

LIFE AND CORRESPONDENCE

OF

MAJOR-GENERAL

SIR ISAAC BROCK, K.B.

INTERSPERSED WITH

.NOTICES OF THE CELEBRATED INDIAN CHIEF, TECUMSEH;

AND COMPRISING

BRIEF MEMOIRS OF DANIEL DE LISLE BROCK, ESQ.; LIEUTENANT
E. W. TUPPER, R.N., AND COLONEL W. DE VIC TUPPER,

" What booteth it to have been rich alive ?
What to be great ? What to be glorious ?
If after death no token doth survive
Of former being in this mortal house,
But sleeps in dust, dead and inglorious!"

SPENCER's "Ruins of Time."

EDITED BY HIS NEPHEW,

FERDINAND BROCK TUPPER, ESQ.

LONDON:

SIMPKIN, MARSHALL & Co.

GUERNSEY: H. REDSTONE.

1845.

Ferdinand based his memoir of Isaac on letters
from a box – left unopened for thirty years.
But where were the letters Isaac had written
during his first three years in the Canadas?

them but, earlier this year, with his mind beginning to wander, Elizabeth had opened the trunks and the box. Isaac's uniforms were moth-eaten but this did not concern her. What did concern her was that someone should write a memoir based on the letters, and she had decided it would be Ferdinand.

At this he smiled, for she was known to be as decisive as the grandmother he had never met: Elizabeth De Lisle Brock. When he protested that he was neither a historian nor a writer, his mother Elizabeth struck the floor with the finial of her walking stick. It had an ivory piqué handle, a burgundy wristcord, and a shaft of Indian Malacca. She reminded him that, while eight of her ten brothers had lived to adulthood, there was not a single Guernseyman left whose last name was Brock. And she would not have Isaac's name tarnished by the memoirs of lesser men.

Pleading exhaustion from his travels, Ferdinand put his mother off. But when Savery died in early August, Ferdinand saw the importance of his task and set to work. It was not a joyous task. When he was not reading, writing, and editing, he helped his mother care for his father, who lay dying upstairs. It was also a frustrating task because Ferdinand could be indecisive. What, for instance, should he do with family lore that his Uncle Isaac had been engaged to a woman named Susan Shaw, a daughter of General Aeneas Shaw? Or that she still lived, as a maiden aunt, in the house of one of her sisters, a Mrs. John Baldwin? In the end, Ferdinand decided not to mention Miss Shaw at all, not even in a footnote.

∽

When the book appeared in January of 1845, Ferdinand was not happy with it. Nor was Elizabeth, even if, for once, she did not say so. In April 1847, when the expanded second edition appeared, Ferdinand was still unhappy. It was bad enough that his Uncle Isaac had rarely noted details about his personal life. Even when he had, one found oneself reading between the lines.

Take the letter that Isaac wrote in London on November 26, 1799 to his eldest brother, John, who was still twenty months away from his fatal duel. In this letter, Isaac described his regiment's role in an invasion that had taken place earlier that autumn. The French had established a puppet regime called the Batavian Republic in the Netherlands. Britain had thought that, if she and Russia invaded northern Holland, the Dutch would rise up against their French masters and restore William of Orange to his throne. The allies were wrong. The invasion began in late August, dragged on till late October, and soured relations between Britain and Russia for years to come.

Toward the end of the letter, Isaac wrote about one of the more successful attacks of the campaign. Two hours before dawn, a brigade led by General Sir John Moore began its advance on the town of Egmont-aan-Zee, which the British called Egmont-op-Zee. The town was on the Helder Peninsula, with its sand dunes, dikes, and windmills. Moore's brigade consisted of four regiments, among them the 49th; and, as the regiment's senior lieutenant-colonel, Isaac led it into battle.

After describing the advance across the sand dunes, he wrote to John:

...I got knocked down soon after the enemy began to retreat, but never quitted the field, and returned to my duty in less than half an hour....

Ferdinand shook his head over the letter because Isaac sounded so casual about the incident.

∽

On Wednesday, October 2, 1799, four days before Isaac's thirtieth birthday, he nearly died. Again. First the fever, now this. He did not count the duel because he had not been in real danger on that Barbadian beach. So he now told himself. Nor did he count that first impulsive swim to Castle Cornet. Still, here he was, nearly thirty, and he had cheated death twice.

In his darker moments, it seemed to him that the whole reason for living was to keep cheating death till it dealt a hand no mortal – and certainly no soldier – could trump. At such times, Isaac thought of the two boys and two girls his mother had buried; of his brother, Ferdinand, who had not lived to see his twentieth birthday; and of their father, John, who had died on foreign soil just as Isaac nearly had, moments ago – not in Brittany but in north Holland. And not while taking the waters but while inspecting what he had thought was safe ground.

Isaac swore he would never make that mistake again.

Shortly after the enemy began to retreat, he was surveying the battlefield from his saddle. Had the land been more flat – not broken up by dunes – he could have seen farther than the windmills off to his left.

They reminded him of windmills he had seen in Barbados. Here they pumped water; there they worked machinery that crushed sugar cane. He anchored his feet in the stirrups, rose from his saddle, and squinted at the next line of dunes. This was when an invisible hand sliced into his throat.

Even as he toppled from his saddle, he dropped his sword. He rolled down the dune with his lips pursed and his eyes shut to keep out the sand. Unlike the warm and powdery Caribbean sand, this was cold and gritty North Sea sand. He came to rest partway down the dune, tried to rise to his knees, and fell onto his side. With his left hand, he tried to brush grit from his face. With his sword hand, he held his throat as though this could help him breathe; but where that invisible hand had nearly sliced off his head, now it was choking him.

Two soldiers dropped their muskets and picked him up. They shouted at one another; they shouted for the surgeon. With the sand always threatening to give way, Isaac thought they might drop him at every step. Yet somehow they carried him to safety and laid him in the shelter of a dune. They left him, ran back to retrieve their muskets – which they should not have dropped – and then returned. One man reloaded while standing guard. The other ran off again, this time shouting for Dobson, who was nowhere near the front of this strange, irregular battlefield. Why would he be? He was a private servant, not a soldier.

Isaac was grateful, but he wished that the man watching over him would move away. Isaac needed room to breathe. Staring up at a spinning grey sky, he tried to calm his pounding heart.

The last time he had been in Holland, he had been fourteen, then fifteen. Half a lifetime ago. Not in north Holland; neither in Bergen nor Amsterdam, where the people were fair-haired and blue-eyed. He had been in south Holland, in Rotterdam, where the people had been darker. But north or south, the Dutch had one thing in common: men were ruggedly handsome and women had healthy good looks. Like the maid who had worked next door to Père Jean's house, where Isaac had lived. She had been fifteen, then sixteen, and she had taught him about love. Not spiritual love. The other kind, the one that had mattered more to him then. And still did now, if and when he allowed himself to think of it. She had taught him well and her name had been –

Annoyed, he shook his head. He had once heard that when the memory goes, the mind cannot be far behind. But he was still young, four days short of thirty. He was too young to go mad and far too young to die. He closed his eyes so he would not have to look at the spinning grey sky. What had happened to him? Why did he feel so weak? And why could he barely move?

It had been his mother's idea that he live in Rotterdam that year. She had wanted him to learn proper French – not the patois he used in the streets – and so she had written to a Protestant clergyman, a friend of a friend, and he had agreed to teach Isaac after he finished at school in Southampton. This clergyman, a Frenchman, went by the name of Père Jean. Isaac smiled. Had his mother realized what she was doing by sending him to live with a man named Father John? And they did live less like master and student than like father and son. Père Jean had a resonant voice.

He went on and on – about the Dutch, their stories, their struggle with the devil in the sea – while Isaac listened and learned. For a year he spoke only French. And a certain amount of Dutch, though he lost this.

Now he heard a sound that was out of place among the sounds of battle. It was the clucking of a tongue. He opened his eyes to see his brother Savery looking down at him. Isaac raised his head and glared. Trust Savery to cluck like a broody hen.

Isaac waved Savery away, then lowered his head once more, but his brother would not leave. Isaac sighed loudly, then smiled again. Whenever he looked at Savery, he saw himself four years younger: the same lean build; the same large head of fair hair; and the same blue-grey eyes. But their uniforms told them apart, as did their age, for Savery's coat bore far less braid than Isaac's. Nor would Savery earn any more braid till he learned to be less impetuous.

By rights, he should have been a lieutenant-commander in the Royal Navy but, like their father, he had never risen beyond midshipman. John had left the navy for the peaceful life of a gentleman. Savery had been forced to leave.

Eight years before, in 1791, he had signed a petition that had condemned the punishment of midshipmen by mastheading. On a calm day, it was pleasant to climb to the top of a foremast, tie oneself to the masthead, and sit there for hours – even if a fall to the forecastle could break one's neck. But in rough weather mastheading was hell. No matter how tightly the poor young man tied himself to the mast, every moment brought the fear of death. There he sat, in pouring rain or driving snow, while the masthead corkscrewed up, down, sideways.

But the petition by itself had not led to Savery's downfall. So to speak. What had incensed his superior officers had been his audacity – and that of his fellow midshipmen – in making a round robin. They had signed their names in a circle so that their superiors could not guess who had first signed his name. Who might be singled out as their ringleader. And so Savery had been given a choice: he could remain a midshipman for the rest of his naval career, or he could resign and join the army. He had chosen the army. Sometimes Isaac was glad of this. At other times – earlier this morning, for instance – he was not.

As a paymaster attached to the brigade, Savery was exempt from action. But, impetuous as always, he rode his horse to the front, then rode from the top of one sand dune to the top of the next and urged the men on. At last, and Isaac wondered why it had taken so long, Savery's horse was shot out from under him. After picking himself up and slapping the sand off his uniform, he strode past Isaac. At this Isaac bellowed, "By the Lord Harry, Master Savery, did I not order you, unless you remained with the general, to stay with your iron chest? Go back to it, sir, immediately!"

Savery shot back, with a smile, "Mind your regiment, Master Isaac. You would not have me quit the field now?"

The retort left Isaac speechless. The men nearby knew better than to laugh but he guessed that, by nightfall, the story would spread through the regiment. For all his adherence to discipline, he would be seen as truly concerned for his fellow men. For blood brothers, for brothers in arms.

He closed his eyes once more. He heard Savery questioning the soldier who had remained on guard. The man replied with phrases like *clutched at his throat* and *no sign of blood*. Bored, Isaac listened instead to the voice of Père Jean, which, after all these years, he heard as clearly as a bell.

How Isaac had enjoyed the fables. How he had laughed while Père Jean had told him about Chanticleer, the rooster; Grimbert, the badger; Reynaert, the fox. Brock meant badger, as Père Jean well knew. The fables made fun of the rich and even the clergy. Only the Catholic clergy, Père Jean said.

But the story of the bells – that had been Père Jean's favourite. He claimed that the Dutch, for all their cleverness at building dikes and dams and sluices, often found it difficult to work together. As for working with Belgians, this was impossible. Isaac did not know whether to believe his teacher, but he was so well read that he seemed to know everything. He said no one knew who had invented the story of the bells – a Belgian, the Dutch claimed – but it began like this:

Once there was a Flemish philosopher named Kwiebe-Kwiebus. He arrived in a Dutch town of one hundred districts, each having its own belfry and its own bell. While he travelled in this town, he noticed that the people of each district knew little about the people of neighbouring districts. Nor did they care to learn. In each district, he heard the same question: "Is our bell not unique?" There was more to the story, but Isaac could not remember the rest. He did remember that Père Jean had repeated the story many times before Isaac understood first the words, then the moral of the story. And he repeated it many more times before Père Jean was satisfied with his pronunciation. Without thinking, Isaac now blurted, "The bells." His voice croaked. He opened his eyes in time to see Savery frowning at him as though Isaac had gone mad. "Kwiebe," Isaac croaked. "Kwiebus." When he tried to laugh, he sounded like a frog. Savery looked even more worried. Isaac shook his head and again closed his eyes.

His throat hurt less now. A few minutes more, and he would be fine. When he gestured with his right hand, he felt someone close that hand around the hilt of his sword. He opened his eyes to see Savery kneeling beside him. Only when Isaac croaked his thanks did Savery rise. Then Savery wondered aloud where Dobson might be. What was taking the surgeon so long? And why was there no blood? Isaac shrugged to himself. Although he still did not know what had happened to him, he no longer needed his servant or the surgeon. Strength was returning to his limbs.

There was so much he had forgotten about that year in Rotterdam, and it had been the happiest year of his life. So much he had begun to recall now that he was back in Holland. Eating in the street: raw herring with onions, smoked eel. Pilgrims and Jews. Lessons in history and art. The *Gouden Eeuw*, the Golden Century, during which the Dutch had built a thousand ships a year. Rembrandt and Vermeer. And, always, the cleanliness. Every Saturday was *schoonmaakdag* – clean-making day – when people took soap, water, and brush to the steps and walks in front of their houses.

That was when he had first seen her, the maiden, or so he had thought, whose name was –

He felt hands at his throat. Instinctively, he pushed the hands away. He opened his eyes to see Dobson, kneeling while he unwound the handkerchief at Isaac's throat, then the black cravat. Dobson's eyes widened. When he pressed a fingertip gently on the curve below Isaac's Adam's apple, Isaac flinched. Dobson muttered his apologies and rose.

Isaac turned onto his stomach, raised himself onto his hands and knees, and then, by using his sword like a crutch, regained his feet. Dobson moved to catch him when he staggered, but Isaac waved him off. Then he bent to retrieve his hat. Straightening, he croaked, "By the Lord Harry, what's become of my horse?" He scowled at the grins on the faces of the two soldiers. He ignored Savery's impish smile and the tears in Dobson's eyes.

∽

Ferdinand put down the letter from Isaac to John, then recalled what little he knew about the rest of the campaign.

The battle for Egmont-op-Zee had continued and the 49th paid a high price. Of the nearly 400 men of the regiment in the field that day, thirty were killed, fifty were wounded, another thirty went missing. On Wednesday and Thursday night, the 49th camped on the sand hills without shelter; with only biscuits to eat. Biscuits sodden by the rain. Then the regiment entered Egmont, and on Saturday it marched into Alkmaar. Here, on Sunday, Isaac celebrated his thirtieth birthday. By the end of October, with the weather worsening, the British and Russians withdrew.

The 49th returned to England, and in late November Isaac wrote the letter to John. Of the action at Egmont, he said,

> ...I had every reason to be satisfied with the conduct of both officers and men, and no commanding officer could be more handsomely supported than I was on that day, ever glorious to the 49th....

Some lines later, despite his annoyance with Savery, Isaac praised him. Between these two passages, Isaac mentioned that he had been knocked down but soon returned to duty. Worried, John wrote to Savery, who replied,

> ...Isaac was wounded and his life was in all probability preserved by the stout cotton handkerchief which, as the air was very cold, he wore over a thick black silk cravat, both of which were perforated by a bullet, and which prevented it entering his neck. The violence of the blow, however, was so great as to stun and dismount him, and his holsters were also shot through....

It occurred to Ferdinand while he reread these lines that Savery could have added, "Isaac leads a truly charmed life." But knowing Savery – impetuous, impious – Ferdinand suspected that he would have added, "'Tis a good thing Master Isaac, like a true gentleman, is rarely without his handkerchief."

Horatio Nelson often posed without the patch that hid his blind eye. Painted by John Hoppner in 1801, the year Isaac met England's heaven-born admiral at the Battle of Copenhagen.

4

With Nelson at Copenhagen

In late February of 1801, a year before Isaac would be posted to Upper Canada, he found himself on a ship of the line called the *Ganges*. The 760 men of his regiment were spread among the fifty-three ships of a huge fleet, and with him on the *Ganges* were the regimental band and the light company – elite soldiers trained in skirmishing and marksmanship. Also with him, as in north Holland, was his gallant brother Savery.

The fleet was sailing from the south of England toward the Baltic Sea; toward Denmark and Russia. These two nations, with Sweden and Prussia, had formed the League of Armed Neutrality. France now had an uncrowned king – her First Consul, Napoleon Bonaparte – and the League was playing into his hands by closing the Baltic Sea to Britain. She needed timber, flax, and hemp for her navy, and so this fleet planned to teach the Danes a lesson. If Denmark refused to leave the League, the British would capture the Danish capital of Copenhagen. This was no idle threat, for leading one of the squadrons that comprised the fleet – the squadron that included the *Ganges* – was the man Britain called her heaven-born admiral: Horatio Nelson himself.

Even Isaac, who was not a sailor, knew that this was a bad time of year for such an expedition. The *Ganges* sailed through snow, sleet, and fog. Ice coated spars and rigging. Each morning, sailors climbed the rigging and, with their hands tied in rags, cleared snow off the spars. It fell onto the upper decks. From here, soldiers and sailors tossed the snow into the sea. Many of the sailors, fresh from the warm Mediterranean, shivered and coughed. Too many of Isaac's men were also falling ill. And, while crossing the North Sea, the *Ganges* had to tack continually because the winds were from the northeast. By the time they reached Copenhagen, Isaac knew, the soldiers and sailors would be demoralized, frozen stiff, or both.

He shared his thoughts only with the captain of the *Ganges*, Thomas Fremantle. Fremantle agreed. As the seniormost officers on board, the two quickly became friends. Each night, after the other officers left the captain's table, Isaac and Fremantle chatted while sipping their second glasses of port.

Fremantle revealed that he had been with Nelson at the Battle of Tenerife – in Spain's Canary Islands, off the northwest coast of Africa – four years before. Fremantle had thought he might lose an injured arm but had not. Nelson had been less fortunate. Not only had his right arm been amputated above the elbow, but it had also taken ages to heal. Even now the stump – what Nelson called his fin – twitched when he grew nervous or excited. Imagine, Fremantle told Isaac. Nelson had one arm and one eye. He was prone to fevers from malaria and to seasickness. He had been promoted so quickly that he had never mastered navigation or seamanship; yet here he was, at forty-two, not only a vice-admiral but also Britain's darling.

As Isaac saw, this did not prevent the other officers from gossiping over dinner – though, because their captain was one of Nelson's band of brothers, they were careful not to go too far. They were intrigued by Nelson's affair with Emma, Lady Hamilton, the young wife of an elderly diplomat. This affair was the worst kept secret in the Royal Navy. Why, rumour had it that Lady Hamilton had recently given birth to a daughter named Horatia – perhaps even to twins – but everyone pretended this was malicious gossip sown by Nelson's enemies. After all, he was married, and his wife Frances had borne him no children.

Later, alone with Fremantle, Isaac laughed at the captain's stories about life at sea. He was a likable man. He was shorter than Isaac, as were most men, and pudgier than Isaac would have expected of a military man. Then again, many of Nelson's officers were pudgier than Isaac had expected. No one commented on this because these officers were among the finest sailors in the world. And, unlike most admirals, Nelson insisted that his officers and men eat well in order to remain healthy. Among them was Captain William Bligh of the *Glatton*.

Two years before, Bligh had lost a ship called the *Bounty*. Its crew, led by Fletcher Christian, had mutinied near Tahiti and set Bligh with a handful of loyal men adrift in a longboat. He had done the impossible: he had sailed the open boat more than 6,000 kilometres and brought his men safely to port. What was a little pudginess compared with such daring? Such skill.

And yet Isaac insisted that the light company and the band exercise. No matter what the weather, each day he led the men in brisk walks along the upper decks of the *Ganges*. He knew that the men grumbled, but he also knew they liked showing off their discipline to the cold and weary sailors.

Now he looked fondly at Fremantle. The captain made no bones about missing his wife, Betsey, or their three children – all of whom had been born during the first three years of Fremantle and Betsey's marriage. He wrote her long and frequent letters. Isaac suspected he had been described in detail – especially his habit of knocking his head on the low beams of the *Ganges*. Each night, even as Isaac left the table, Fremantle reached for paper, pen, and ink.

Headed for his own cramped quarters, Isaac wondered what it must be like to have a wife and children waiting at home. He soon dismissed the thought. He was not even thirty-two, some four years younger than his new friend. There was plenty of time to find a wife and father children; yet he already knew what he would name his first son.

Isaac's grandfather had been a William, and so was
Isaac's eldest Uncle Brock. Isaac's father had been a
John, and so was Isaac's eldest brother. If Isaac followed family tradition – and why would he not? – he
would name his own first son after himself. But what
he could not guess was the name of his future wife.
Susan, perhaps, or Mary. Then there was his mother's
name: Elizabeth. A fine name, that.

∞

On the morning of Thursday, April 2, 1801, Isaac
paced the quarterdeck of the *Ganges*. He watched
Thomas Fremantle gesture with a card while confer-
ring with his officers. They nodded and dispersed into
blurs of blue coats and white piping. Then Fremantle
glanced once more at the card. It had been delivered at
dawn by Thomas Foley, Nelson's flag captain on the
Elephant. Foley looked older than Fremantle, and
though the two captains appeared to be friends, their
camaraderie seemed forced. After Foley left,
Fremantle felt obliged to tell Isaac why: they had more
in common than their Christian names, for Foley had
courted Betsey before she had become Fremantle's
wife. The mother of his children.

Now Isaac shook his head over how tangled lives
could become. He saw Fremantle frown at the card
once more. It was a simple and ingenious device,
invented by Nelson. Because the smoke of battle could
obscure signal flags, the card bore Fremantle's orders
for the day. These orders had been settled the night
before, at a gathering of captains aboard the *Elephant*.

Isaac had not been invited because he was not the seniormost army officer with the fleet. Lieutenant-Colonel William Stewart had this honour, and so he sailed with Nelson. Isaac admired Stewart – not because he was a Member of Parliament but because, like Nelson, Stewart was an innovative officer. After studying Austrian tactics, he had formed the Experimental Rifle Corps, whose 100 officers and men also sailed with the fleet. Hoping that his corps would be made a proper regiment, he had already designed its uniforms: not scarlet like the uniforms of the 49th and other regular regiments but a dark, rifle green. Isaac wondered whether the British army would ever accept such unconventional dress, but Stewart seemed confident that it would. Nelson called him the rising hope of the army and Isaac promised himself that, before long, others would say the same about him.

After returning from the *Elephant*, Fremantle had told Isaac about the gathering. It was a tradition Nelson observed on the eve of every battle. The vice-admiral had been in such high spirits, he had proposed a toast for a leading wind and success in battle. Now it seemed that Nelson's first wish was coming true, for the winds were from south by southeast. The skies were cloudy and the weather moderate. As for his second wish – success in battle – it would come true only if his plan of attack worked as well in practice as it did on paper.

Twelve ships of the line, among them the *Ganges* and the *Elephant*, were anchored at the southern end of a body of water called the King's Channel. They would soon sail north along the channel, which was bounded on the east by a shoal called the Middle Ground. Along the western shore of the channel, defending the wharves of Copenhagen, waited Danish ships with their masts and rigging removed. And floating batteries: row upon row of guns. Isaac counted twenty-five ships and batteries, in all. Beyond rose church spires and, beyond them, hills. Through a junior officer's telescope, he spied spectators gathering on rooftops and church towers. He saw coats and fur hats and fancied that the ladies looked back at him through opera glasses.

He dismissed the fancy and reviewed the orders for the day. While sailing parallel to the Danish ships and batteries, Nelson's squadron would pound them into submission. After this, as Isaac had explained to his officers over breakfast, the 49th would go into action.

Accompanied by 500 sailors under Fremantle, the 49th would storm ashore at the northern end of the King's Channel. Here the men would take the Trekroner Battery, the dreaded Three Crowns Battery, with its seventy guns. The orders were simple enough, and his officers nodded. They looked grim. During the month it had taken the British fleet to cross the North Sea, sail south through a strait called the Kattegat and then into the Øresund, the Gold Sound that separated Denmark from Sweden – during all this time, the Danes had strengthened their defences. So a British envoy had reported, after he had gone ashore some days before to once again demand that Denmark quit the League of Armed Neutrality. The Danish Crown Prince had refused.

Isaac's officers wished one another luck. Then they left for their ships to relay his orders to ensigns and sergeants major. Savery remained at the table. Impetuous as ever, he insisted on accompanying Isaac when the 49th stormed ashore.

"Is it not enough that one brother should be killed?" Isaac demanded. Yet Savery persisted till Isaac waved him off. Shortly afterward, Isaac climbed to the quarterdeck and had a word with Fremantle. "Pray, leave it to me," the captain said.

A few minutes later, Savery also appeared from below deck. His scowl vanished when Fremantle called out, "Master Savery, you simply must remain with us. I appoint you captain of the gun. It will amuse you."

Now, Savery looked happy to be commanding the quarterdeck gun. He had once been a midshipman, after all. His first love was still the sea. And, Isaac thought, this should keep him out of harm's way. Yet Isaac could not help worrying. He remembered what his eldest brother, John, had once said. True, brothers could look out for one another, but no one was impervious in war. Not even a Brock. Suddenly, Isaac heard cheers. Looking at his pocket watch, he saw that it was almost 9:30. Then he looked toward the *Elephant*. Nelson was signalling the long-awaited order: weigh anchor and attack.

During the next four hours, Isaac often checked his pocket watch and shook his head with disbelief. At times, it felt as though time was speeding by. At other times, it seemed to slow. Then again, as he knew from Holland, time passed strangely during a battle – in ways that defied the very laws of nature.

⚭

Nelson's attack began badly. Three of his ships ran aground onto shoals. Then the remaining nine ships tried to put into action a plan that required his having all twelve.

The plan would still have worked had the pilots who steered his ships up the King's Channel not been afraid of going aground. They were Englishmen and Scots who plied the Baltic trade in tobacco, timber, and hemp. They were not fighting men. Fremantle shouted at his pilot to steer closer to the Danish line. The pilot refused. Even as Fremantle cursed him, a round of shot took off the man's arm. He slumped to the deck. Worse, the round killed the ship's master outright. Still cursing, Fremantle took the helm. He cast Isaac a glance that said, "Heaven help us."

At 10:00, the *Ganges* followed the *Elephant*. After Captain Foley brought her to rest across from the flagship *Dannebrog*, in the centre of the Danish line, Fremantle steered the *Ganges* starboard of the *Elephant*. He then veered to port. He brought the *Ganges* to rest half a cable length – about ninety metres – in front of the *Elephant* and ordered the stern anchor dropped. Then the *Monarch*, under Captain James R. Mosse, followed suit. She passed to starboard of the *Ganges*, also veered to port, and also tried to anchor half a cable length in front. But the *Monarch* went too far. She anchored within range of the Trekroner Battery and, later, Isaac learned that Mosse was among the *Monarch*'s first casualties. He died with his speaking trumpet in his right hand and his card of orders in his left. His men threw a flag over his body and continued the fight.

With the *Ganges* shuddering under Isaac's feet from the firing of her port guns, he strolled to the starboad railing. From here he watched Fremantle, who had given up the helm to the master's mate, shouting orders. Isaac read Fremantle's thoughts when he shook his head. Most of the British ships were anchoring too far from the Danish line. And because the floating batteries lay low to the water, they made difficult targets. Also, the Danes were better gunners than anyone had expected.

In London, newspaper artists did not caricature the Danes as they did the French because the British thought of the Danes as brothers who had been deluded by Bonaparte. But now the Danes were fighting for their lives; for Copenhagen and their honour. Worse yet, they could reinforce their positions with men who rowed out from the wharves. But the rest of the British fleet – including the ships that drew too much water to navigate the King's Channel – remained safe to the northeast of the Middle Ground shoal. There, Isaac knew, Sir Hyde Parker, the cautious admiral who commanded the fleet, could only watch while Danish fire decimated Nelson's squadron.

Nelson, Britain's impetuous darling.

Isaac glanced at his watch. It was now 11:30, and the carefully orchestrated battle had become a melee. He looked astern at the *Elephant*. She was trading fire with the *Dannebrog* and two floating batteries. Bodies floated face down among splintered debris. It seemed to him that he was watching not a battle but a slugging match. Ships of the line? Floating batteries? They were two files of boxers trading blow for blow with neither side willing or able to yield.

He winced when yet another round of grapeshot shredded the mainsails of the *Ganges*. Then he heard a whoosh and turned – in time to see Savery, hunched over his cannon, knocked onto his back.

Running toward his brother, Isaac cried, "Ah, poor Savery is killed!" Down on one knee, Isaac clasped Savery's hand. Almost at once, Savery opened his eyes. He looked stunned. Before Isaac could say more, Savery struggled to his feet. He rubbed his head and returned to his gun. Only then did Isaac realize what had happened: grapeshot had passed so close to Savery that the heated air around the shot had knocked him off his feet.

Isaac returned to the starboard rail and continued to pace.

He could barely see the spires now, because smoke was drifting off the King's Channel and onto the wharves. He could barely see the spectators. But he could see the flashes of gunfire from the Danish ships and floating batteries. He could hear the cries of men, Britons and Danes, felled by shot. The sand that had been spread to improve footing on the *Ganges'* decks was red with blood. Here a sailor tried to pull a splinter out of his thigh. A splinter the size of a stake. There, a sailor sagged against a mast with his left arm, torn off at the shoulder, lying at his feet. And caught in the rigging of the mainmast were an upper torso with arms and head and a lower torso with legs – the remains of a man sliced in two by a cannonball. His guts oozed down the rigging like skinned rats.

Isaac began to feel queasy.

Below decks, he knew, sweat ran into the head-bands worn by the gunners. Their ears bled from the concussions of their cannon. And in the after cockpit, below the waterline, the surgeon was hard at work. Here, on what normally served as the midshipmen's dining table, he sliced and stitched. Laid out on a tray were his pincers and tongs, his knives and saws. On the far side of the table stood a glowing brazier in which he warmed his instruments. Next to it stood a large wooden bucket into which he threw amputated limbs. By now his leather tourniquets were slick with blood. Beside him, the chaplain muttered prayers even as he poured rum down the throats of wounded men. The rum would lessen the pain. Or perhaps, Isaac thought, this feeble anaesthetic served another purpose: if the men had to die of shock from loss of blood, at least they could die half drunk.

He shuddered.

He squeezed his eyes to shut the pictures out of his mind. When he breathed deeply to calm himself, he breathed gunpowder and salt air. He thought he might choke. Hopeless, it was bloody hopeless. And he was useless till the ships ahead of the *Ganges*, the *Monarch* among them, could silence the Trekroner Battery. But the battery and, now, two Danish ships were shredding her sails. So much for the *Monarch*. He wondered when he could finally storm ashore with his men and with Fremantle's sailors. Those who could still fight.

As it turned out, Isaac never had the chance.

At 1:00 in the afternoon, Admiral Parker's flagship hoisted signal 39, the order to leave off action. Isaac and Fremantle turned to the *Elephant*. She was still trading fire with the *Dannebrog* and the two floating batteries, and the *Elephant* still flew Nelson's favourite signal, number 16: close action. Later, Isaac would hear from Lieutenant-Colonel Stewart what was happening on the quarterdeck of the *Elephant*. For now, Isaac watched Fremantle scoff at signal 39. With all the smoke drifting across the shallows of the Middle Ground, Admiral Parker could not see what Fremantle and Isaac could plainly see: they were wearing down the Danes.

By 2:00 in the afternoon, fighting had become sporadic. The *Dannebrog* was on fire and had slipped her moorings. Her men were jumping into the water before she could explode. The flames had leapt to other ships and poured down onto floating batteries. A wall of burning timber faced the *Ganges* – a wall that began at the *Dannebrog* and spread north along the Danish line.

At 3:30, according to Isaac's pocket watch, the *Dannebrog* exploded and sank. From all along the line came the cheering of British sailors and soldiers, but the cheers were halfhearted. He looked at Savery, who grinned while wiping his sleeve across his sooty face. Isaac pulled out his handkerchief and dabbed at the soot on his own face. Then he glanced at Fremantle, who looked drained of his usual vigour. Fremantle shook his head as if to say, "Some victory this is turning out to be."

∽

During the voyage out from England, Fremantle had more than once said that he would introduce Isaac to Nelson. Now sailors rowed Fremantle and Isaac to the *Elephant*, which they boarded safely from starboard. Fremantle led Isaac onto the quarterdeck.

Naval captains clustered about Nelson while Lieutenant-Colonel Stewart stood to one side. He was the only other officer nearby in a scarlet coat. When Isaac touched his hat, neither Nelson nor his flag captain, Foley, returned the salute. Stewart did this for them. While Fremantle joined his brother officers, Isaac joined Stewart at the port rail. From here they watched the remnants of the *Dannebrog* bobbing in the water while British sailors pulled Danes – prisoners, now – into boats.

Isaac and Stewart exchanged news, mostly about casualties. Full reports had not yet come in but the toll would be high: over 250 killed, nearly 700 wounded. Soldiers as well as sailors. The only consolation, and it was a consolation for a military man like Isaac, was that Danish casualties would number in the thousands. Now, though, Stewart told Isaac something that made him furious. One of their officers, instead of keeping his men safe below decks, had ordered them to stand to attention at the gangway as a lesson in bravery to the Danes. They had not been impressed. They had mowed the soldiers down with grapeshot. When Isaac demanded to know the officer's name, Stewart said there would be plenty of time for reckoning later. Then, as if to divert his attention, Stewart told him what had happened after Admiral Parker's flagship had flown signal 39:

"Lord Nelson was at this time, as he had been during the whole action, walking the starboard side of the quarterdeck. A shot through the main mast knocked a few splinters about us. He observed to me, with a smile, 'It is warm work, and this day may be the last to any of us at any moment.' Then, stopping short at the gangway, he said with emotion, 'But mark you, I would not be elsewhere for thousands.'" Stewart kept his voice low so that it would not carry to Nelson or his captains.

When Isaac chuckled, he, too, tried to keep his voice low. He knew exactly how Nelson must have felt. The battle had been dreadful and Isaac felt exhilarated at having survived.

Stewart had not finished. "When signal 39 was made, the signal lieutenant reported it to him. He continued his walk, and did not appear to take notice of it. After a turn or two he said to me, 'Do you know what's shown on board of the Commander-in-Chief, number 39?' And when I enquired of him what that meant, he answered, 'Why, to leave off action. Leave off action!' he repeated, and then added, 'Now damn me if I do!'"

Isaac laughed loudly, and one of the captains glanced at him. Stewart placed a hand on Isaac's cuff to draw him nearer, then continued, still in a low voice:

"Some moments later, Nelson turned to his flag captain, Foley, and said, 'You know, Foley, I have only one eye. I have a right to be blind sometimes.' Then, placing his pocket telescope to his blind eye, he said, 'I really do not see the signal.'"

Both Isaac and Stewart burst into laughter. Stewart, sputtering, repeated, "'I really do not see the signal!'"

Suddenly, the captains around Nelson parted, and Isaac found Nelson frowning at him. Isaac straightened his sword at his side and touched his hat. Instead of returning the salute, Nelson continued to frown. His features relaxed only when Fremantle announced, "My lord, may I have the honour to present Lieutenant-Colonel Brock? Commander of the 49th Foot."

Nelson's lips pursed as though the name meant nothing to him. Then he turned back to his captains. Isaac could see that the vice-admiral had much on his mind.

And so he did. The British sailors who were trying to pluck Danes out of the water were being fired on from the shore. Some of the Danish ships, though reduced to hulks, were firing again – now on the British who were trying to board. This was what Nelson and his captains were discussing.

Even as they parted once more, Isaac saw Nelson nod. He said angrily, "Either I must send on shore and stop these irregular proceedings, or send in our fire ships." Then he called to his purser, a Thomas Wallis, for paper, pen, and ink. Nelson reminded the officers present of what he had told Sir Hyde Parker when the admiral had sent the British envoy to the Danish Crown Prince. "I hate your pen and ink men," Nelson had said. "A fleet of British men-of-war are the best negotiators in Europe." Now he declared that pen and ink were needed, after all.

Isaac watched Nelson write a note while Wallis, standing close, made a good copy because Nelson had never learned to write neatly with his left hand. Finished, he read the note aloud while his captains murmured in agreement. He raised his voice to carry over the sound of guns that still fired from ships and shore.

"To the brothers of Englishmen, the Danes," the vice-admiral read, "Lord Nelson has directions to spare Denmark when no longer resisting; but if the firing is continued on the part of Denmark, Lord Nelson will be obliged to set on fire all the floating batteries he has taken, without having the power of saving the brave Danes who have defended them. Dated on board His Britannic Majesty's Ship *Elephant*, Copenhagen Roads, April 2nd, 1801. Signed, et cetera, et cetera."

When Isaac pointed out to Stewart that the British had taken few of the floating batteries, Stewart reminded him that the Danish Crown Prince did not know this.

Isaac chuckled once more. He knew that he was watching history being made; that Nelson had just written one of his most famous letters. But how could Isaac know that, with his passion for applying the lessons he learned, he would one day send a similar ultimatum to another enemy? At a faraway post called Fort Detroit. Or that he would send this ultimatum to an American general whose forces would outnumber Isaac's by two to one.

After Nelson signed the neat copy of the letter and Wallis folded it for him, the purser moved to seal it with a gummed wafer. Nelson stopped him. He wanted the letter sealed properly, with wax. And so Wallis ordered a sailor to go below; to fetch a candle, a stick of red wax, and the vice-admiral's seal. While Nelson waited, he paced. And while he paced, Isaac examined him.

Nelson was shorter than Isaac – shorter, even, than Captain Foley, who towered over him each time Nelson passed close by. But he was not a short man. It was difficult to tell while he paced, but he could have been anywhere from 162 centimetres to 167 centimetres tall. Anywhere from five feet, four inches to five feet, six inches. He also looked as if he weighed no more than sixty kilograms. His face was pale and his eyes, deeply set under thick eyebrows, were bloodshot as though he had barely slept during the night.

The *Elephant* shuddered even as shots struck amidships. No one else seemed to notice and so Isaac continued his examination.

Nelson's wide mouth looked too sensitive for a tenacious warrior. Most surprising of all, his voice was nasal and high-pitched. He spoke as if he thought no one listened to him. Or as if he thought that no one believed he was serious. Even in his vice-admiral's finery, he looked as though he was dressed for a play. A red sash crossed his blue coat, and the star of the Order of Bath glittered above his left breast. About his neck he wore medals, but they failed to distract Isaac from Nelson's other souvenirs of battle. A black patch covered his blind right eye; his right sleeve was pinned to his lapel; and the stump of this arm – his fin – twitched.

When Isaac frowned toward Fremantle, the captain shrugged as if to say, "He still doesn't feel that he's won." And Isaac knew that the British would not win till the last Danish gun fell silent.

Now Wallis, the purser, turned from the ladder-way leading down from the quarterdeck. He suggested that Nelson use the gummed wafer, after all. When Nelson demanded to know why, Wallis explained that the sailor he had sent below had had his head blown off by a cannonball. At this, Nelson ordered, "Send another messenger for the wax," and so Wallis did.

Isaac glanced at Stewart, who shrugged.

When Isaac looked away from Stewart, he found himself face to face with Nelson – if this were possible, given that Isaac stood a head taller than the vice-admiral. Nelson was scowling at Isaac as if he had broken wind. He did not know what to say. Then Fremantle stepped forward. Even as he explained that Isaac was a Guernseyman – like his uncle, Captain Sir James Saumarez – Nelson's face brightened.

To dispel any chance of misunderstanding, Isaac admitted that he was James's nephew by marriage, not by blood. After this Isaac and Nelson chatted freely, though Nelson did most of the talking. And talked mostly about himself.

He reminisced about his superb victory at the Battle of the Nile, two and a half years before. Then, at Abukir Bay, he had destroyed Bonaparte's dream of conquering Egypt and marching on India. Foley had been there, as captain of the *Goliath*; so had Saumarez, as captain of the *Orion*. Nelson mused, "I recall Sir James as erect and – shall we say? – supercilious. Is he still so?"

Thinking of his Aunt Susan, Isaac laughed. She would have bristled to hear her brother described as haughtily disdainful. Isaac replied, "Yes, my lord. Pride and good posture are hallmarks of the Saumarez line. As they are of all Guernseymen."

Nelson exclaimed, "Well said, my good Colonel, er –?"

"Brock, my lord. Isaac Brock."

But Nelson was already turning away. "Wallis," he demanded, "what is taking that infernal messenger so long?" The purser turned from the ladderway and showed what he held: the candle, the wax, and Nelson's seal. Isaac watched while Wallis, after lighting the candle, melted red wax onto the seam of the letter. Then, with Nelson's seal – silver and ivory and bearing his coat of arms – Wallis finished with the letter. He handed it to a Commander Frederick Thesiger, an officer who spoke Danish. Thesiger left for shore in the *Elephant's* gig – Captain Foley's boat – with a flag of truce tied to an oar and held aloft by a sailor. After this, Nelson seemed to relax and yet, from time to time, his stump twitched in his right sleeve.

Isaac wanted to ask Nelson something, but he doubted that his kinship with Sir James Saumarez would allow this. When he looked at Stewart, he saw that Stewart ached to ask the very same question. And so, Isaac let his superior take the risk.

"My lord," Stewart said, "may I ask why, under so hot a fire and after so lamentable an incident" – he was referring to the first messenger, who had been killed by the cannonball – "you should have been so particular about the wax?"

At this, Nelson turned upon Stewart, and even Isaac could not help stiffening to attention. He stood at ease when Nelson nodded as if to say, "Fair question."

"Had I made use of a wafer," he said at last, "it would have been still wet when the letter was presented to the Crown Prince. He would have inferred that the letter was sent off in a hurry, and that we had some very pressing reasons for being in a hurry." Nelson drew himself up with his left arm behind his back. He was still addressing Stewart but looking at Isaac. The vice-admiral finished his lesson with, "The wax told no tales."

Association of Canadian Map Libraries and Archives. Facsimile Map Series, Map no. 144 (ISSN 0827-8024)

The theatre of war in North America. From the old Northwest to the Eastern Seaboard, the War of 1812 would become a sideshow to the real war in Europe. Or so people thought.

5

Home from the Canadas

On Monday, October 21, 1805, shortly after Isaac turned thirty-six, the Royal Navy won the greatest sea battle of the Napoleonic Wars. Off a Spanish cape called Trafalgar, near the Strait of Gibraltar, a British fleet led by Horatio Nelson defeated a fleet of French and Spanish ships. Even as the battle began, Nelson composed a signal that took thirty-one coloured flags to send. It would become his most famous signal, and it read, "England expects that every man will do his duty." Then he saved Britain from Napoleon. Or so people claimed.

Isaac knew better, but he kept his opinion to himself because, in winning the Battle of Trafalgar, Nelson had paid the ultimate price. Dressed in his admiral's finery, pacing with his new flag captain on the quarterdeck of HMS *Victory*, Nelson had made an easy target for marksmen in the rigging of French ships. A musketball entered his shoulder, passed through his chest, and shattered his spine. He died some hours later but not before learning he had won the day. The day, the decade, and the century.

Isaac did not know whether to laugh or cry. Nor did his fellow Guernseymen. They stopped one another in the street to exclaim, "Boney's done for now!" Then they burst into tears.

Long before Nelson's body reached London for a state funeral at St. Paul's Cathedral, there was talk of erecting a Nelson Monument – a statue that would soar on a column in the middle of London. Isaac hoped that he, too, might one day die such a glorious death; that his own words might inspire a nation; and that a Brock Monument might one day mark his own, great deeds. At the moment, all he had to show for the past few years was his recent promotion to full colonel. Three and a half dreary years in a colony on the edge of the world. In the Canadas.

Still, he and Dobson were home once again, and Isaac planned to enjoy his leave. He had hoped to spend an entire year in Guernsey and England, but this would not be. Thanks to the Americans. Thanks to the people his mother had called filthy, rebellious rabble.

They were no longer satisfied with having won their independence from the British Crown. Now they felt that Britain did not take their new country seriously. And so a group of men called the War Hawks had hit on a simple solution. Add Upper and Lower Canada to the Union. Add Nova Scotia and New Brunswick. Even Cape Breton and Prince Edward Island. Add six new, shining stars to the Stars and Stripes. Then see how long Britain, strangled by her aristocracy, would sneer at America, where all men were created equal. Except African slaves, of course. And women. After all, Americans claimed, Africans were practically animals. No better than beasts of burden. And women were not men.

Isaac spent part of his leave at the fine granite house in St. Peter Port. These days another Elizabeth ran the house: his eldest sister, who had been named for their mother. Elizabeth De Lisle Brock had died ten years before, in 1795, the year Isaac had bought his commission as a major. Now her body lay in the parish churchyard while her spirit danced with the spirit of her beloved husband, John.

Isaac's sister Elizabeth had also married a John – John E. Tupper, Esq. – and, though she was only fifty, she enjoyed her role as matriarch of the Brocks. She spoke often about her sons, of whom there were so many that Isaac could not remember their names let alone their ranks or regiments or ships. Among these sons were another John E., a Charles, an E. William, and a William De Vic. Still at home were the youngest children: a boy, Ferdinand, and a girl, Henrietta. Ferdinand intrigued Isaac because, unlike most boys, Ferdinand had no interest in swords or ships or uniforms. Like Henrietta, he prized books, and so Isaac asked the children to help him choose the books he would take back to Upper Canada. The choices filled an entire trunk, and his niece and nephew delighted in reciting the titles at dinner.

Henrietta: "*Oeuvres Militaires* by Guibert."

Ferdinand: "Gregory's *Dictionary of Arts and Sciences.*"

Henrietta: "*Réglement de l'Infanterie.*"

Ferdinand: "Plutarch's *Lives of the Artists* and *Lives of the Saints.*"

Henrietta, to her parents: "And a new literary journal called *Edinburgh Review.*" Puzzled, she added, "We're Guernseymen, Uncle Isaac. Not hielan' Scots!"

After dinner, he and his brother-in-law, John E., retired to the parlour for their port. Isaac opened the Guernsey *Star*, stretched his long legs toward the fire, and tried to read. Outside, southwesterly gales drummed at curtained windows. John filled and lit his clay pipe. He offered to fill one for Isaac, and Isaac refused because he had never developed the habit. Then John asked about life in the Canadas. Isaac sighed, not too loudly, and put the newspaper down. He regularly wrote to his brothers, and at some length; but, in his rare letters to his sisters, he said little beyond assuring them that he was well and enquiring after their children. Now Isaac began halfheartedly and yet, while he spoke, he warmed to his subject.

He gave his impressions of life in the North American colonies, and he spoke of random events. Not about all of them, though. Not about the desertions or the mutiny. Certainly not about the horribly botched execution.

∽

Shortly after the 49th arrived in the Canadas, in June of 1802, Isaac sensed trouble in the ranks. This was nothing new – there was always trouble in the ranks – and a commanding officer had to worry only if his soldiers stopped grumbling. Besides, soldiers had much to grumble about. Most men died not from wounds but from disease. There were so few barracks that, when the regiment was stationed in England or the Channel Islands, the men were billeted at inns. Here they slept two and three to a bed. As for marriage, only six men in each company were allowed wives, and married couples lived in a part of the barracks that was screened off by a blanket.

Then there was the food. The women did the laundry, the men cooked, and a soldier who did not grumble about his food could not be trusted. Each man's daily ration was two-thirds of a kilogram of bread; half a kilo of beef, which the men usually boiled; and a litre of ale. Many Irishmen enlisted because beef, even if the ration did include the bone, was better than potatoes every day. Still, few officers felt sorry for the men. Some were criminals, many were poor and, like the officers, the men drank far too often and far too much. Only discipline could keep such men in order. Discipline and punishment.

For the smallest infraction, a man was flogged with a whip called the cat. Its nine tails were dipped in brine to heighten the pain. First he was stripped to the waist, then tied facing a triangle made of spontoons. These were short pikes: three vertical pikes tied to form a triangle, with a fourth tied horizontally at waist height. A drummer, supervised by the drum major, did the flogging – anywhere from 300 to 700 lashes with the cat. If the man fainted, or if the regimental surgeon thought his life was in danger, the man was cut down. Some weeks later, he received the rest of his punishment – after the maggots were picked from his unhealed flesh.

Isaac was not fond of the cat and so, if a man was sentenced to 200 lashes for losing his razor and stealing one from another man, Isaac would commute the sentence to 100 lashes. On the other hand, if a man was sentenced to 200 lashes for being drunk before morning parade, Isaac reduced the sentence by only fifty lashes. He could not abide drunkenness.

While some of his officers muttered about his soft heart, he knew he had the loyalty of his men. Like Dobson, they would follow him anywhere. Within a few years of having become the 49th's senior lieutenant-colonel, Isaac had turned it from one of the worst regiments in the army into one of the best. The Duke of York, the commander-in-chief himself, had said this. And so, while neither Isaac nor the 49th looked forward to their transfer to the Canadas, he expected the men to give their new posting a chance. Besides, the beauty of the Canadas could stir the most jaded soul. So people said, and so it proved.

While sailing up the St. Lawrence River, Isaac marvelled at the cliffs and banks, the stretches of forest. And the city of Quebec, built where the Rivière St. Charles joined the St. Lawrence, here narrowed by islands like Île d'Orléans – why, Quebec was even more picturesque than St. Peter Port.

Gazing up Cap Diamant, which rose nearly 100 metres from the river, he could see why it was called the Gibraltar of North America. Quebec was impregnable. Here, in 1690, thirty-two ships had brought 2,000 British soldiers. Their leader, Sir William Phips, had demanded that the governor, Comte de Frontenac, surrender New France – to which Frontenac replied he had no answer but what he could give with the mouths of his cannon. Here, too, Governor Sir Guy Carleton had repelled an invasion at the beginning of the American Revolution. Nearly twenty years before this, in 1759, Carleton had been a colonel in the forces led by General James Wolfe against French forces led by the Marquis de Montcalm. Wolfe had been mortally wounded but, like Nelson, Wolfe had lived long enough to learn he had won. Montcalm had died of his wounds the next day, at an Ursuline convent. This battle, fought on the Plains of Abraham during the Seven Years' War, had changed the face of North America.

Isaac's men did not have his appreciation for history. Why would they? Few of them could read and write, and this was why he looked favourably on those who could. Among them was a man named Carr, and one day Isaac noted the surliness of Carr's salute. After ordering another of his favourites, Sergeant Major FitzGibbon, to bring Carr to him, Isaac accused Carr of planning to desert with other men as soon as ice covered the St. Lawrence. To flee to the United States.

When Carr denied this, Isaac stepped forward with his fist clenched. "Don't prevaricate," he said. "Tell me the truth, like a man. You know I have always treated you kindly!" After Carr confessed, Isaac told him, "Go, then. Go and tell those deluded men all that has passed here. I will still treat every one of you with kindness, and you may then all desert from me if you please." FitzGibbon looked appalled at Isaac's choice of words, and he dismissed both men with a scowl. Only one man deserted, in September, before ice covered the river. He was the only man Isaac lost to desertion in those three and a half years in the Canadas. And, though this still rankled, he had one consolation: the deserter was not Carr.

∞

During Isaac's leave, he also stayed with an elder brother, William, who lived in London with his wife, Sally. William was a merchant in the Baltic trade that had once been threatened by the League of Armed Neutrality. He took an interest in his brothers' careers. He had loaned Isaac money to buy his early commissions and hoped that their youngest brother, Irving, might one day also become a merchant. But Irving had little stomach for the trade, beset as it was by French privateers, and he feared financial ruin. He dreamed of retranslating the memoirs of a seventeenth-century writer named François Bernier and of calling this book *Travels in the Mogul Empire.* Irving's two volumes would not be published for another eleven years, but his retranslation would become a classic.

As for Savery, he had less interest in commerce than Irving did. Savery had not enjoyed his position as a paymaster and so, when the 49th had left for the Canadas, he had exchanged into another regiment in the hope of seeing action. Three years from now, in 1808, he would serve as an aide-de-camp in the

Peninsular Wars. After the death of General Sir John Moore at La Coruña in northwest Spain, Savery would return to St. Peter Port, marry, and become a colonel in the militia. His son, Julius, would die in boyhood.

Isaac and William enjoyed talking about their brothers and sisters, and Sally often joined in. Though she sounded cheery when the talk turned to nieces and nephews, Isaac heard sadness in her voice because she and William had no children. Isaac and William spoke of this only when they were alone. After they retired to the parlour with their port, Sally waited half an hour. She supervised the servants' clearing away and washing up before joining the men.

What troubled William, besides Sally's attempts to bear their disappointment quietly, was that there were too few children in the family with the last name of Brock. Worse yet, there were too few boys, and with the taste for adventure that ran in Brock blood, too many of these boys were dying young. Usually in uniform. Looking suddenly aghast, William glanced at Isaac, but Isaac nodded in agreement. He had often thought of this but never said so in his letters home. His brothers read the letters to their wives, and the wives read the letters aloud to entertain friends at tea. Isaac gazed at the fire while William poured himself a second glass of port. In the flames, Isaac saw what he knew of the past and present and what he hoped for the future. The future of a family named Brock.

Ferdinand had gone first and left neither a widow nor heirs. John had gone next and also left no heirs. The third brother, Daniel, had only two children: a son and a daughter. The son, Eugene, was an officer in the

20th Regiment and the daughter, whose name Isaac could not recall, was still unmarried. So was Isaac. So were Savery and Irving. No wonder Elizabeth, bless her, insisted that young Ferdinand call himself not a Tupper but a Brock Tupper.

Isaac understood the importance of names. Take Daniel's. Seven years before, he had been elected a jurat – a councillor – of Guernsey's royal court. He often travelled to London and to St. Helier, in Jersey, to defend Guernsey's privileges in trade. He hoped to become lieutenant bailiff of Guernsey, as their De Lisle grandfather had been. And so, over the years, Daniel Brock came to be known as Daniel De Lisle Brock and then as Daniel De Lisle.

At least he still looked like a Brock. When Isaac had visited him in St. Peter Port – Daniel had let Elizabeth have their parents' house and built himself a fine new one – Isaac had thought he was looking at a mirror that showed him the future. This was just how he would look in seven years: the same blue-grey eyes; the same large head that poets described as leonine. But there were telling differences: Daniel was shorter than Isaac and, like William, Daniel was thick about the waist.

Isaac looked up from the fire to see William leaning against the mantel. William was looking at Isaac as though he alone might leave sons who would also leave sons; as though he alone could save the family name. Before he could laugh off William's serious manner, Sally entered the room. She looked idly at a copy of the Guernsey *Star*, which John E. Tupper had sent to William through Isaac. After setting down the paper, she took up her needlework. She was embroidering a silhouette of Isaac, who watched her fondly till she startled him by asking how long it would take to defeat Bonaparte. She called him Boney, as many Londoners still did – although the year before, in December of 1804, he had crowned himself Napoleon, Emperor of France.

∞

Early in January 1806, while Isaac was in London, he met with the army's commander-in-chief in his offices at the Horse Guards. The building was in Whitehall, north of Westminster Abbey. Aides hurried to and fro in these corridors of power. Even in his best uniform, Isaac felt shabby in the presence of so much glitter. He counted three stars of the Order of Bath.

Then there were the swords. There were Highland broadswords with basket hilts. There were sabres whose blades were so curved that they were useless in battle. He smiled to think how, after he had become an ensign, he had spent hours practising salutes with the ornate spadroon. He had practised so much that he had nearly worn out the scabbard. Now he bore a simple infantry sword he had bought ten years before – with its gilded hilt and folding shell-guards; with its leather scabbard also fitted with gilt. Dobson had shone these till they gleamed, but here, at the Horse Guards, the gilt seemed as dull as a sermon.

Then there were all the mirrors. Here, a guards officer fiddled with the curving points of his waxed moustache. There, an ensign made sure that his single epaulette hung just so. Isaac forced himself to ignore the mirrors so he would not fidget with his uniform. Surrounded by all this finery, he longed to return to the field. Even more, he longed to return to the Canadas. For three and a half years, he had been homesick for Britain; yet now that he was back, he found himself thinking often of the Canadas. How best to defend them.

At last, an aide led Isaac into a posh office, its walls hung with paintings of former commanders-in-chief. The meeting began with chat, most of which concerned Nelson – who, the army insisted, had not saved Britain. Napoleon had, by breaking up his camp at Boulogne-sur-Mer, where his *Grande Armée* – a quarter million strong – had been preparing to cross the Strait of Dover. He had broken up the camp to march eastward and defeat the Austrians – first at Ulm, without firing a shot; then, six weeks after Trafalgar, at Austerlitz. Now he was building an *Arc de Triomphe* in the middle of Paris. The gall of the man.

After the chat, Isaac delivered his report to the Duke of York. An aide, Lieutenant-Colonel Gordon, took notes.

The formal part of Isaac's report was brief. He pointed out that, after the revolution, Americans who had settled in the Canadas had received grants of land. As their name implied, these United Empire Loyalists could be counted on to remain loyal to the Crown. But now the Canadas were being overrun by Americans who were hungry for land yet felt no loyalty to the Crown. At the same time, British soldiers were deserting to the United States because of opportunities to be had there. Like all soldiers who claimed to have no interest in politics, Isaac spoke at length about politics. Especially about the rabble-rousing War Hawks.

Then he made his proposal. First, he said, create a veteran batallion whose members would be rewarded for their service with grants of land. Next, garrison this batallion at Quebec. At posts like Kingston and York, garrison only soldiers who were least likely to desert. Finally, depending on how long each man served in the veteran batallion, give him up to 80 hectares of land.

After delivering his report, Isaac sat back and listened while the other senior officers discussed his proposal. As so often happened, crucial information came out during the less formal part of the meeting. When asked about the state of defences in the Canadas, Isaac replied that Quebec and Kingston might be able to repel an invasion if their fortifications were strengthened, but all the other posts might fall. These included Fort George and Fort Erie, between Lakes Ontario and Erie; Amherstburg and Sandwich, between Lakes Erie and St. Clair; and York itself, the poorly defended capital of Upper Canada.

He sat back once more and listened to the discussion without seeming eager about its outcome. He looked at the pale January light creeping in through the high windows. Then he noticed the Duke of York eyeing him and looked away. The Duke also sat back from the long oak table – to give his belly room to expand when he breathed. Isaac reminded himself to be kind.

The Duke of York was the second and favourite son of King George III. Mad King George, his subjects called him. The Duke had become a major-general by twenty. He had twice led disastrous invasions of the Netherlands – the second time, only six years before, when Isaac had been knocked off his horse. Though the Duke was a likable man, his blunders in the field had made him a laughingstock. And yet he had had the last laugh, because after his appointment as commander-in-chief, he had shown a flair for administration and army reform. Such things mattered to progressive men like Isaac, for whom the pace of reform often felt as dreary as the pace of a funeral march.

In his personal life, the Duke was still the butt of jokes. He gambled and he chased women. At least he was not as reckless as some of his brothers.

Five years before Isaac had been posted to Barbados, another of George's sons, Prince William Henry, had arrived in Bridgetown as commander of the frigate *Pegasus*. While in port, he and his friends had visited the Bay Street establishment of Rachel Pringle Polgreen. She was a legend in the Windward Isles: a woman so huge, with a cleavage so deep, that a man could lose his head. She called her place a hotel but every young officer knew it for what it was. And, though she tried to act like a lady, she would always be a madam. One evening, the Prince and his friends were in such high spirits that they smashed all the furniture and fittings. Before the *Pegasus* left port, Rachel sent him a bill for 700 pounds. With this money, she refurnished her place and renamed it – the Royal Navy Hotel.

As for the Duke of York, he was embarrassed not only by his brothers but also by his wife, Princess Frederika of Prussia. She was famous for three things:

she had a short, dumpy figure; a plain face; and bad teeth. No wonder the Duke, like his elder brother, the Prince of Wales – soon to become Prince Regent – kept a mistress. Rumour had it that the Duke's mistress made a fine profit by trafficking in officers' commissions, or was that the mistress of –?

Isaac realized that the Duke was looking straight at him. That the Duke was, in fact, asking a question Isaac had hoped someone would ask:

"What might you propose should these United States invade our Canadas? Speaking *entre nous,* of course, my dear sir."

"Your grace," Isaac replied, "I might propose two distinct yet related courses of action." He told the room at large, "*Entre nous.*" Then he tried to ignore all the eyes upon him. The guarded eyes of other senior officers in the room; the unblinking eyes of former commanders-in-chief. "First," he said, "I should repel the invasion with all the forces I could muster."

"And then?" asked Lieutenant-Colonel Gordon, looking up from his notes.

Even the portraits seemed to be holding their breaths while Isaac wondered whether to take a chance. But there was more at stake here than his own good name or his hope of further promotion. "And then?" he said at last. He risked a polite shrug, for he was merely saying what was on every mind, though not on every tongue: "I should invade the United States."

Looking from Fort Niagara toward Fort George, could the Americans see Isaac arresting the mutineers? Those who planned a slow, unpleasant death for his second-in-command.

6

Desertion and Mutiny

Sally had warned Isaac not to be late for lunch – she was inviting some influential friends she wanted him to meet – but he told William's driver to circle St. James Park. Slowly. The cool drizzle that beaded on Isaac's hat and dampened his greatcoat suited his mood, as did the open carriage. It turned from Parliament Street onto Great George Street.

The meeting at the Horse Guards had gone well. Perhaps too well. Even as it had ended, the Duke had been in a jovial mood. He had clapped Isaac on the back and exclaimed that he hoped to hear of no more midnight boat rides. The officers present had laughed. So had Isaac, though he had inwardly cursed. He should have known that everyone at the Horse Guards would have heard of his one and only reprimand. It had come from Lieutenant-General Peter Hunter, who had been commanding the forces in the Canadas. All for taking action where a timid man would have balked.

It could have been worse, Isaac reminded himself. The Duke might have mentioned the mutiny and the execution. Still, midnight boat rides, indeed.

∽

By the summer of 1803, a year after arriving in Upper Canada, Isaac was stationed at the barracks of York, on the northwest shore of Lake Ontario. He lived in one of a number of wooden cottages that were little more than huts. The barracks stood some three kilometres west of the so-called town. He hoped to build a proper fort one day. For now, he contented himself with having built a blockhouse, its second storey projecting over its first; a powder magazine; and a ditch that encircled the barracks and Government House. He kept the elite light company of the 49th at these barracks and stationed the rest of the regiment at Fort George, on the southwest shore of the lake. There, close to the mouth of the Niagara River, his men kept watch on the Americans in Youngstown, on the opposite bank. Also at York were men of the 41st Foot. He would blame them for what happened early in that long, trying summer. Mostly, though, he would blame himself.

Shortly after midnight, Dobson woke Isaac to say that Sergeant Major FitzGibbon was sounding the alarm. Dobson was in his nightshirt. While Isaac dressed, FitzGibbon made his report from the doorway. He had just learned from the sergeant of the watch that three of his men were missing. So was a bateau and the sentry who should have been guarding the boat sheds. Isaac ordered FitzGibbon to gather a sergeant and twelve privates and ready another bateau. Next, Isaac ordered the roll to be called in the barrack rooms.

Soon, the captain of the light company made his own report: three more men were missing. So was a corporal of the 41st, an artificer or craftsman. From what the captain could learn, this corporal had convinced the other six men to desert.

By 12:30 Isaac was striding angrily down to the water. Here he climbed into the bateau and ordered the men to push off. Then he pointed southeast by south and ordered them to row. The sergeant kept a lookout at the pointed bow while, at the pointed stern, Isaac and FitzGibbon agreed on a course of action once they reached the south shore.

Isaac looked about and shook his head. He would have preferred a canoe – one of the large canoes used by fur traders that could carry thirty men – but the army insisted on using bateaux. In some ways, they were useful: twelve metres long, two and a half metres wide, a bateau could carry about four tonnes of cargo. A movable mast rose from its midst and from the yard hung a squarish sail. A lugsail. A bateau moved well before the wind but sailed poorly if the wind changed course. There was no wind that night, and so the men rowed – six for one hour, six for the next. The oars were so long that the men had to rise to their feet while they pulled. So it went, six men resting near the useless mast while the other six bobbed up and down. While Isaac tried to sleep.

He could not sleep, though. He was feeling the excitement of the chase; of doing what no soldier, to his knowledge, had yet done: cross Lake Ontario in an open boat. When FitzGibbon insisted that Isaac rest, he huddled in the pointed stern and closed his eyes. The bateau rocked and creaked. He opened his eyes to see FitzGibbon silhouetted against the stars. Even Dobson admired the sergeant major, and Dobson was not easily awed. He had been with Isaac for twelve years now, FitzGibbon for half that time, and Isaac treasured them both.

FitzGibbon's Christian name was James. Isaac never called him this even if, at times, he seemed like a younger brother. Not impetuous. Not like Savery. But, though FitzGibbon was a Catholic, Isaac trusted him as he would a blood brother.

FitzGibbon was twenty-three. He had been born in a stone house near Glin, in County Limerick. The town stood inland from the Mouth of the Shannon on the west coast of Ireland. At fifteen, he had joined the local yeomanry and, three years later, left Ireland for England with the Tarbert Fencibles. He dreamt of becoming an officer – so he later told Isaac – but, unlike Isaac, FitzGibbon had neither money nor influence. However, he did know how to read and write. This impressed a visiting general, who urged him to join the forces being amassed to invade Holland. Later that year, five months shy of his nineteenth birthday,

FitzGibbon found himself a sergeant in the 49th Foot. His life since then had been one adventure after another. He was captured at the Battle of Egmont-op-Zee and spent three months in captivity until the British and French exchanged prisoners. A year later, during the expedition to Denmark, FitzGibbon set sail with his grenadier company on the *St. George* but the company soon moved to the *Monarch*, captained by James R. Mosse. At Copenhagen FitzGibbon watched the *Monarch* pounded by the Trekroner Battery. Over fifty men died, Mosse early on; over 150 were wounded; and yet FitzGibbon emerged unscathed. Except for the memory of cannon fire, Isaac supposed. The shrieks of the dying, the putrid smells of the dead.

A year later, while the 49th sailed from England to the Canadas, Isaac was walking the deck when he heard a sneeze. He found FitzGibbon lying in the boat that hung over the ship's stern. When Isaac asked FitzGibbon what he was doing, he held up a manual, *The Rules and Regulations for the Field Exercises of His Majesty's Forces*. Laughing, Isaac walked away. When the 49th reached Quebec and the post of sergeant major came vacant, Isaac promoted FitzGibbon over the heads of forty older sergeants. Still, the fellow had much to learn.

One day recently, Isaac had asked him why he had not carried out a simple order and FitzGibbon had replied it was impossible. "By the Lord Harry, sir," Isaac said, "do not tell me it is impossible! Nothing should be impossible to a soldier. The word *impossible* should not be found in a soldier's dictionary!" Now Isaac could not remember what the order had been, but he knew that FitzGibbon had learned his lesson. One day, Isaac promised himself, he would get the sergeant major his commission.

At last Isaac fell asleep. Moments later, it seemed, he woke to find FitzGibbon shaking him. It was nearly fifty kilometres from York to Niagara, near Fort George. It was morning, and the men had rowed all night.

At Niagara, Isaac ordered a Lieutenant Chesshire to take some of his men in a bateau along the American shore, east of the Niagara River. Meanwhile, Isaac returned to York by a long route. His bateau followed the south shore of the lake and then, where the lake rounded to a point overlooked by the Burlington Heights, followed the north shore to York. He thought it unlikely that the deserters were still in Upper Canada, but he had to eliminate the possibility. He and FitzGibbon, with the sergeant and twelve privates, reached York by nightfall. Isaac was hungry, but Lieutenant-General Hunter wanted to see him. At once.

It was Isaac's bad luck that Hunter was at the barracks that week instead of at Quebec. Hunter reprimanded him for having crossed the lake in an open boat. He told Isaac that he should not have been so rash. It was one thing to risk other men's lives, but a commanding officer should not risk his own. Isaac silently disagreed. Dismissed, he ate a cold supper brought by Dobson and fell exhausted into bed.

Earlier in the day, across the lake, the adventure – as Isaac described it in a letter to a fellow officer – had come to a curious end. None of Isaac's letters from these early years in the Canadas would survive, but the end of this adventure would become a part of colonial army lore:

Lieutenant Chesshire and his men rowed their bateau east along the American shore of the lake. With them was a native scout. At one point he asked whether he could land to shoot some game and Chesshire agreed – as long as he stayed within sight of the bateau. Soon the scout glimpsed a red coat among the trees. He called to Chesshire, who landed with his men, and they marched, sweating, through the woods. After a while, the lieutenant called a halt so his men could drink from the lake. Two deserters, also thirsty, appeared at the edge of the water. Before long, Chesshire had all of them in irons.

Lost in his memories, and startled by the driver's asking, "Home, sir?" Isaac wondered whose home this might be.

The carriage had circled St. James Park but he had seen nothing – not even wildfowl in the pond. At least the drizzle had stopped. "Yes, home," he replied. He felt oddly heavy and realized his greatcoat was soaking wet. He sighed. When his home was not a barracks hut, it was a ship's cabin or the house of a sister or brother. Then again, he was neither a merchant like William nor a gentleman like John E. Tupper. Isaac was a soldier, he lived a soldier's life, and, God willing, he would die a soldier's death.

Not like those fools who had deserted. Or the men who had later planned the mutiny. That was no way for a soldier to die.

∽

From London, Isaac and Dobson took a boat up the Thames to Pangbourne, in Berkshire, and then a coach to Compton, where Isaac's other sister, Mary, lived. During the journey, Dobson marvelled at how close English towns seemed. Compared to the Canadas, he said, Britain felt tiny to him now. Isaac agreed. Overland, it was nearly 300 kilometres from Quebec to Montreal. That journey took three days at breakneck speed with many changes of horse. This journey was a leisurely one; yet in no time at all, it seemed, Isaac reached Compton.

Like Elizabeth, Mary had married a gentleman, Thomas Potenger, Esq., whose first cousin was the Countess of Bridgewater. Mary and Thomas had three children: a boy, William, and two girls, Maria and Zelia. William hoped to join the 22nd Regiment – the Cheshire Regiment, with its pale buff facings and gold lace. His sisters were learning to be ladies.

Isaac adored the girls and they adored him. When they asked about the natives of the Canadas – Maria called them Red Indians; Zelia called them savages – he admitted that he knew very little about them. Except that they all looked alike, just as the African slaves in Barbados had all looked alike. Would the girls like to hear about fur traders instead? Oh, yes, they would. And so, while they practised their needlework in front of the fire, he told stories that left them open mouthed. He taught them foreign words and exotic names: muskeg, portage; Michilimackinac; voyageurs, Métis, coureurs de bois.

Before leaving Compton, he asked the girls what they might like him to send from the Canadas. Both of them asked for muffs made of the finest skins. Four years later, Dobson would still be trying to find these skins for Isaac to send. He wanted nothing but the best for his nieces, and no skins he saw would do. By then, Mary assured him in a letter, the girls had forgotten his promise. Just as – and she hesitated to write this, but she knew he would understand – they barely remembered his visit.

∞

No matter where Isaac went in that autumn, winter, and spring of 1805 and 1806 – whether in Guernsey or England – he felt as if he was being followed.

At first he found this humorous. Then he found it unnerving because he was being followed by a man he had never met. People kept asking whether he had heard of Major-General Sir Arthur Wellesley. Yes, Isaac said, he had now; and, though he did not say so, he was tired of hearing about him. Wellesley had been born in 1769, the same year as Isaac and, by coincidence, the same year as Napoleon. Now they were all thirty-six. Wellesley was the latest, rising hope of the British army; Napoleon was Emperor of France; Isaac was a mere colonel. A colonial, at that, or so he thought of himself when he forgot his accomplishments. His dreams of a glorious future.

Wellesley had been born into a family that, unlike the Brocks and De Lisles, contributed little to society beyond collecting rents and filling minor government posts. The Wellesleys had gained their Irish lands during the time of Good Queen Bess, but rumour had it that Wellesley's eldest brother, the Earl of Mornington, was a pauper. And so he cajoled what he could not buy. Thanks to the Earl, young Arthur had served as aide-de-camp to three Lords Lieutenant of Ireland and then, at twenty-one, had become a Member of the Irish Parliament. Still, he was a gentleman, and Isaac approved of this – just as he approved of Wellesley's musical training, his poise in the saddle, his footwork in the dance.

What Isaac could not abide was Wellesley's apparent lack of commitment. The man was a butterfly. He had flitted from regiment to regiment and wasted a fortune buying uniforms. There was more. He was quick to lose his temper and swore like a trooper. None of these qualities impressed Isaac, who forgot that, when he lost his own temper, he yelled, "By the Lord Harry, sir!"

To give Wellesley his due, though, he had shown he was not just another Anglo-Irish fop; and he had done it in a colony on the edge of the world. Not in the Canadas but in India.

As Isaac well knew, officers at the Horse Guards turned up their noses at service in India. Fighting brown-skinned savages was nothing like fighting civilized Europeans. On the other hand, an officer could learn much about the art of war in India if he had a talent for leadership – military and civil – which Wellesley proved to have. Best of all, there was more prize money to be had in a single princely state than in all the Canadas. No wonder people with connections at court trafficked in commissions. A senior officer who paid a few thousand pounds for a commission could earn tens of thousands of pounds from his share of the gold and jewels of a defeated native prince.

If the officer lived, that is. In a place as unhealthy as India, Wellesley should have died of gangrene or malaria. Yet, somehow, he had not only survived but also triumphed.

In 1799, he had helped defeat a South Indian Muslim named Tipu Sultan. Crushing Tipu's forces had allowed the British to take Mysore, one of the richest kingdoms in the south. Then there had been other triumphs like the defeat of the proud warrior people called Mahrathas. Wellesley had gone to India in 1796, a year after Isaac had bought his own commission as a major, and returned to Britain in 1805, shortly after Isaac had been promoted to full colonel. Wellesley had left as a lieutenant-colonel and returned as a major-general and a Knight of the Bath.

The final straw came in April of 1806.

Isaac was back in St. Peter Port and staying with Elizabeth's family. She kept gushing about Wellesley's marriage, which every illustrated paper felt obliged to report. Earlier that month, in Dublin, he had married Kitty Pakenham, one of the Earl of Longford's daughters. Rumour had it that, twelve years before, the family had rejected Wellesley because of his lack of a fortune. Now there was no such objection. Rumour also had it that Kitty was no longer the fetching brunette she had once been, and that she suffered from melancholy. But what did this matter? The main thing, as Elizabeth said, was that Wellesley, who would turn thirty-seven in a matter of weeks, had married at last.

She said this while knotting a new burgundy wrist-cord onto an old Malacca walking stick with an ivory piqué handle. To Isaac's relief, John E. Tupper pointed out that there were few daughters of earls in the Canadas and that, for now, Isaac seemed to have little hope of a transfer back to Britain.

The more Elizabeth harped on what Isaac should and should not do, the more he squirmed. What he should do, she said, was to keep applying for transfers out of the Canadas. What he should not do was grow fond of anyone there because the daughter of a colonial could not help him advance his career. What he should do, Elizabeth said, was to get himself command of a regiment that would fight the real fight – in Europe, against Boney – so that Isaac could share in all the prize money to be had. What he should not do was settle for any old regiment like the 49th, even if he had spent years whipping it into shape.

She left the two men speechless – John E. because he did not want to contradict her again, Isaac because everything she said made sense. He had thought about it often during his time in the Canadas. But she did not have to worry about his growing fond of a colonial woman because he had met few who interested him, except as dancing partners. Among them was Susan Shaw, but it would not do for a regular officer to marry the daughter of a militia officer. No matter how charming she was, and Susan could be charming.

So, Isaac nodded at everything Elizabeth said. Then he promised to follow her advice. Not just yet, though, he said. First he had to become a major-general like Sir Arthur Wellesley. Only then would Isaac allow Elizabeth to find him a suitable wife. No doubt Mary could help, through her connection to the Countess of Bridgewater. "There," Elizabeth announced, giving the new wristcord a tug. "That should hold for a while."

∞

Two months later, back in London with William and Sally, Isaac decided to cut his leave short because the news from Europe and America alarmed him. After four recent battles, Napoleon had become the master of Europe. Britain found her trade with the Continent cut off, but Britannia still ruled the waves. This – especially the British practice of stopping American ships to reclaim deserters – was enraging the United States. The War Hawks were looking for any excuse for America to invade the Canadas again. This time there would be no Guy Carleton to beat them back, and even as Britain fought for her survival, she was providing a perfect excuse. On the high seas.

The war would not begin for some time – not for a good five years after HMS *Leopard*, in search of deserters, fired on the USS *Chesapeake* in June of 1807 – but Isaac could not know this. He did know that, if and when the war began, he would teach the Americans a lesson they would never forget. Just as he had once taught those English schoolboys in Southampton how to box.

On June 26, he left London for Milford Haven, a port in South Wales, and then sailed to Cork, on the south coast of Ireland. Here he boarded the *Lady*

Saumarez, a Guernsey privateer bound for Quebec. How fitting, he thought, that he was on a ship named for a member of his extended family. Yet how could he know that he would never see his family again? Watching the Irish coast slip below the grey-green horizon, he sighed. He was looking forward to rejoining the 49th and yet he was not, because commanding a regiment was not at all as glamorous as he had once imagined. After the midnight boat chase, early in the summer of 1803, he had thought that the troubles with his men were over.

How wrong he had been.

∞

One morning in August, Isaac found himself once more crossing the lake with FitzGibbon, this time on a schooner. It had brought an alarming message to York from Fort George. Between the message, what Isaac soon learned, and what would come out at the court-martial, he pieced together the events that had led to the message:

That morning, the servant of a major in the Royal Artillery was crossing the common from Fort George to Niagara when he met a soldier named Fitzpatrick running in the opposite direction. Only one and a half kilometres separated the town from the fort, but the day was hot. Fitzpatrick stopped to ask the servant the time, and the servant told him. "Thank God, I will not be too late for the roll call at dinner," Fitzpatrick exclaimed, "for if I were, that tyrant, Sheaffe, would send me to knapsack drill for a week! But, by God –!"

Muttering now, he continued toward the fort while the servant continued toward Niagara.

Lieutenant-Colonel Roger Sheaffe, in charge of the companies at Fort George, was the regiment's second-in-command. The men detested him. Years before, when Isaac had returned from a short leave, the men had broken into cheers as soon as he had marched onto the parade ground. This had been at St. Helier, in Jersey. He had been so angry at their display of favouritism that he had ordered them confined to barracks for a week. Yet Sheaffe had learned nothing from the incident. Even more than the cat, the black hole was his favourite punishment. The four black holes – dug into the earth near the guardhouse at Fort George – were always in use. Rain and snow fell through their iron grilles to drench the shivering men.

After reaching the artillery major's quarters, the servant told him about the encounter on the common. The major then went to the fort and told Sheaffe, who acted at once. Under his questioning, Fitzpatrick admitted nothing, but he looked so guilty that Sheaffe ordered him locked in a cell attached to the guardhouse. Within minutes, word spread through the fort. Soon a soldier named Daly appeared and made a confession to Sheaffe.

Daly had brought his family over from Ireland and had recently joined the regiment. He was Captain James Dennis's new servant and carried the captain's easel when he rambled the countryside to sketch and paint. When Daly's wife was not looking after their children, she worked as a washerwoman to some of the sergeants. One of them, a man named Clarke, had told

Daly that he and his family would find civilian life in the United States more profitable than army life here. Finally convinced, Daly had attended a number of meetings with Clarke and other conspirators. Among them was a corporal named O'Brien. Their latest meeting had been that morning, at Knox's Tavern in Niagara. Fitzpatrick had been so afraid of missing roll call that he had run back to the fort. But, as everyone knew by now, he had been fool enough to speak to the artillery major's servant.

There was one more thing, Daly said: at this morning's meeting the conspirators had decided that, before they fled, certain officers would die. Sheaffe would be first, and his death would not be pleasant.

After hearing all this, Sheaffe met with his company commanders, who convinced him not to take further action until Isaac could be warned. And so, a few minutes before noon, Isaac found himself striding across the common toward Fort George. It was a low, square fort with earth ramparts and cedar palisades. The barracks had loopholes for muskets, and, though nine-pound guns defended the fort, it was no Castle Cornet. He had ordered FitzGibbon to wait on the schooner till he was summoned. At the fort's east gate, which faced the river, Isaac approached the lone sentry. The sentry called out for the guard to appear and present arms, and who should be commanding the guard that day but Sergeant Clarke and Corporal O'Brien?

Walking the decks of the *Lady Saumarez* now, in search of his sea legs, Isaac could not believe how lucky he had been that day. After his meeting at the Horse

Guards, he had decided an officer needed three qualities to succeed: talent, discipline, and luck. Sheaffe was
somewhat talented and certainly disciplined, but he
was not a lucky man. This was why, Isaac thought,
Sheaffe would remain a lieutenant-colonel. He would
no doubt blame his having been born in New England
for his lack of standing with the old boys in London,
but men like him could always find excuses. Isaac
stopped near the helm. He returned a friendly nod
from the ship's master before setting off again.

While facing the guard at Fort George, it had
never occurred to Isaac that his own life, as well as
Sheaffe's, might be in danger. "Sergeant," Isaac said,
"let your men shoulder arms." After they did, he drew
himself up to his full height. "Come here, Sergeant,"
he ordered. "Lay down your pike." Clarke obeyed. He
looked bewildered, but he also obeyed Isaac's next
order: "Take off your sword and sash, and lay them
down." The men in the guard, sweating in the noonday
sun, looked mystified. Next Isaac ordered, "Corporal
O'Brien, bring a pair of handcuffs, put them on this
sergeant, lock him in one of the cells, and bring me the
key." O'Brien dumbly obeyed. Then Isaac ordered,
"Come here, Corporal, lay down your arms." Then, to a
grenadier, "You, bring another pair of handcuffs, put
them on this corporal, lock him in another cell, and
bring me the key." The grenadier also obeyed.

With Clarke and O'Brien under lock and key next
to the guardhouse, Isaac ordered, "Drummer, beat to
arms."

Even as the drum rolled, a young lieutenant
named Williams emerged from the officers' barracks.

He was holding his sword and belt. Pointing at the guardhouse stairs, Isaac said, "Williams, go and instantly secure Rock, and if he hesitates to obey, cut him down." Until recently, Rock had been a sergeant at Montreal. He had been reduced in rank and transferred to Fort George.

Isaac listened to what happened next. Williams ran up the stairs and called for Rock to come with him. Rock said, "Yes, sir, when I have taken up my arms." Williams cried, "If you touch that musket, I will cut you down!" Isaac heard the scrape of a sword being drawn from a scabbard. "Go down before me," Williams said, and Rock did. Soon the conspirators – twelve, in all – were in irons. A guard of men from the Royal Artillery marched the prisoners to the schooner.

In September, Lieutenant-General Hunter issued two orders Isaac did not like but could not contradict. First, all the mutineers and the seven men who had earlier deserted would be court-martialled in Quebec. So would a man from the 6th Regiment who had been caught trying to desert. Isaac sent the prisoners to Quebec with the guard from the Royal Artillery, under FitzGibbon. Second, Hunter ordered, Sheaffe would act for the prosecution. The twenty men stood no chance. In January, after receiving the results of the court-martial, Hunter passed his sentence. Four mutineers and three deserters would be executed. Except for Daly, who was pardoned thanks to Isaac's intervention, the remaining mutineers and deserters were transported to the West Indies. There they would live out their lives cringing at the thought of yellow fever. Of *vomito negro*.

As for the executions, these were carried out at Quebec early in 1804. Shortly afterward, still at York, Isaac received a detailed report. For the first time since having seen the carnage at Copenhagen, he felt ill. He also felt angry and betrayed, but angry at whom and betrayed by whom, he could not say. He ordered the regiment drawn up on the common near Fort George. In a voice that broke, and with no attempt to hide his tears, he told the regiment what had happened at Quebec.

Even now, grasping the taffrail of the *Lady Saumarez*, he thought he would be ill. He turned to the wind and let the salt air sting his eyes till the tears returned. This was what he had told his regiment:

At 10:15 on the morning of Friday, March 2, a procession left the prison for the execution ground. The column, led by two silent buglers and an advance guard of the 41st Foot, included seven empty coffins, each carried by two men; the fifty-six soldiers of the firing party; and an escort with the condemned men. The three condemned deserters were from the 6th, 41st, and 49th Regiments. All four mutineers were from the 49th: Sergeant Clarke, Corporal O'Brien, Fitzpatrick, and Rock. With them walked four Catholic priests and a Protestant minister. Then came the rest of the column, which included surgeons from the garrison; three pieces of artillery; more men of the 41st Foot; its regimental colours; two flank companies of the 6th Regiment; and seventy unarmed men of the New Brunswick Volunteers.

At the execution ground, the prisoners heard their sentences read aloud. It was now 10:30. They were ordered to kneel on their coffins and pray. For forty-five minutes.

Imagine, Isaac told his regiment. These must have been the longest, most fervent prayers of their lives. Each man wore his undress uniform – his white waistcoat and his white breeches and stockings. Nothing marked the regiment he had dishonoured. Not his shako – his stovepipe cap with its plate of stamped brass bearing his regimental insignia. Not his coat with its facings – deep yellow for the man from the 6th, white for the artificer corporal from the 41st, and full green for the men from the 49th. Nor did Clarke wear the sash and sword or carry the pike that had once distinguished him as a sergeant.

How the men must have shivered. The wind blew from the east, from the St. Lawrence, and snow drifted across the execution ground. When the men were ordered to stand, they rose stiffly. Each stood behind his coffin and wondered what, if anything, the next world might hold for a wretch like him.

It should have been over in seconds, Isaac reminded his men, but it was not. Because something went horribly wrong.

It was now 11:15 on that cold Friday morning. The men in the firing party, in three divisions, should have advanced so that they stood just over seven metres from the prisoners. This did not happen. At a distance of forty-five metres, the sergeants of the firing party ordered their men to make ready. But instead of placing the hammers of their muskets on half cock, forty of the men opened fire. All the prisoners were wounded – one in the stomach – but none died. They fell clutching their wounds. Then the sixteen men who had not yet fired marched up to the prisoners. By now they were writhing on the ground while blood stained the white of their undress; stained the white of the snow. Some of them cried, "Have mercy, Jesu!" All of them stared at the leaden sky. The sixteen men placed the muzzles of their muskets against the breasts of the seven wounded men and fired into their hearts.

Standing there on the common, clutching the report, Isaac looked at his officers. Here was Lieutenant Chesshire, who had recaptured the deserters; Lieutenant Williams, who had disarmed Rock; and the artistic Captain Dennis, whose servant, Daly, had nearly betrayed him. There stood all the men. Isaac did not have to ask how they felt. The chins of older men were quivering while they bit their lips. The cheeks of younger men were wet with tears. Only Sheaffe and FitzGibbon seemed unmoved.

"Since I have had the honour to wear the British uniform," Isaac said at last, "I have never felt grief like this. It pains me to the heart to think that any member of my regiment should have engaged in a conspiracy which has led to their being shot like so many dogs!" Then, with his voice breaking once more, he ordered Sheaffe to dismiss the regiment. Isaac should have then marched off the parade ground, but he remained facing Fort George. Dismissed by their officers, the men moved off silently, back to the fort or toward the pier at Niagara. Here the schooner was waiting to return the light company to York.

Still standing at the taffrail of the *Lady Saumarez*, Isaac could not recall how long he had stood alone on the common. But he did recall that he felt he might crumple under the weight of command. Thirty-six? He had felt fifty-six. When he heard a familiar step, he turned to see Dobson, who reminded him it was time to wash before joining the captain for dinner. Isaac remained at the rail till Dobson shrugged and left.

∞

Isaac looked up to check the trim of the sails. He marvelled at the sleek lines of the privateer. Perhaps he should have joined the navy, after all, he thought. Soon he would be back in the Canadas with nothing to show for his leave except a trunkful of books. During the leave, while he had travelled in England and the Channel Islands, he had felt like a Guernseyman first and a Briton second. Once he reached the Canadas, he would again feel like a Briton first – like an Englishman – and Guernsey would feel far away. As far away as India must feel to Wellesley. Yet Wellesley now had a wife and soon might have children. Certainly, he had a home. Isaac had neither wife nor children. Nor did he have a place, however humble, that he could call home.

He tried to lift his spirits by trying to decide which books to read on the crossing, but he had sunk too far to save himself. He wondered whether anyone else had noticed the obvious: most of the men who had been executed that day had been Catholics, and a number of them had been Irish. Why else had there been four priests and only one minister?

Long ago, in England, Catholics had called Protestants heretics and burned them at the stake.

Then Protestants had called Catholics heretics and burned them at the stake. And then there was the penalty for treason: to be hanged, drawn, and quartered. A man was hanged till he was almost dead. Then his belly was sliced open and his guts pulled out to be burned before his eyes. Only then did the axe fall on his neck. Yet even this was not enough. His body was dismembered and his head spiked on a gate. Such vile things had happened as a matter of course two centuries before. Europeans were civilized now. Or were they? A dozen years ago, the French had erected guillotines for their Reign of Terror. They had beheaded so many people that the blood would never be washed from the cobblestones of Paris. Everyone claimed he wanted justice, yet all he took was revenge.

Then a thought came to Isaac that filled him with such dread that he grasped the taffrail as if it was a lifeline. For here was a question he could ask no one, not even his own brothers. Even to think of it might be a heresy:

What if the red-skinned natives of North America and the brown-skinned natives of India were not truly savages, after all? What if the true savages were still the English? And the French.

An invented portrait by J.W.L. Forster of Isaac in his brigadier's coat – and showing only one side of himself, as he so often did.

7

History in a Time of Unreal War

During a battle, as Isaac knew, time passed in ways that defied the laws of nature. The four hours he had spent pacing on the *Ganges* – they had felt like eternity. Yet time could also slow when he recalled an event many years later.

Take the duel on the beach. No more than a few seconds could have passed between the moment he had pressed the muzzle of his pistol into the captain's brow and the moment the captain had dropped his end of the handkerchief; yet those few seconds now felt as though they had stretched into hours. Isaac knew that, in a sense, they had. Because, over the years, he must have recalled the incident dozens –

perhaps hundreds – of times. He could still see the captain's florid and sweaty brow whitening around the muzzle. And Isaac could still smell the captain's piss while it had run down his breeches. Pooled in the sand beneath his shoes. Isaac had been careful to omit this detail when he had told Susan the story of his one duel. And the smell of piss, as he learned – first in north Holland, later in Copenhagen – was the smell of fear. One of many smells, and he soon learned them all: first sweat; then piss; then shit; then warm, black blood; then, finally, that awful, gaseous smell of spilled guts. And he understood now why, so often in his life, he had been fearless: because, in the heat of battle, he lost his sense of smell. Not completely, because it came and went. This was how he knew that he must have been afraid at Copenhagen: he had smelled gunpowder and salt in the air. And, he now thought, charred oak.

By thirty-nine, Isaac learned that time held even more surprises. It was speeding by, and he knew why this should be. When he had been fifteen, even as he had become an ensign, a single year had stood for one-fifteenth of his life. When he had been thirty, a single year had come to stand for only one-thirtieth of his life. Even as the fraction had halved, the speed with which time passed had doubled. So did the speed with which his own life passed. Or so it seemed. In a few more years he would reach forty-five. Time would pass at double the speed it had when he had been twenty-two, triple the speed it had when he had been fifteen. Soon he would be racing toward old age and death. Far from worrying him, the discovery intrigued him as little else did these days – even if he had finally risen from the senior officers' list to the general officers' list. But brigadier or not, he had to escape the Canadas. For if there was little to intrigue him here, he would advance neither in intellect nor rank. He would end his days as yet another general turned governor – in Quebec, say, among surly habitants and moneygrubbing priests – or in some island paradise like Jamaica, awash in pestilence and rum. Yes, he had to escape to England or Europe because there was not only little to intrigue him in the Canadas but also no one from whom he could learn. He was the finest British officer here. Everyone said so. As he put it to himself one day, while he buttoned his brigadier's coat over his thickening waist, he might soon become the largest fish in this colonial backwater. This picturesque Canadian pond.

And so, while he feigned indifference toward Arthur Wellesley, Isaac longed for a command under Wellesley because he was fighting in a real war. Only he seemed able to bloody Napoleon's nose. Not that Wellesley was always victorious, but even as Nelson's immortal memory lingered in British hearts, Wellesley replaced the heaven-born admiral in British minds.

In the late summer of 1807, Wellesley commanded a brigade in yet another British expedition to Copenhagen and defeated a small Danish force near the town of Kiöge. The following spring, recently promoted to lieutenant-general and given command of 12,000 men, he began trying to free Portugal from Napoleon's grasp. In the late summer of 1808, helped by the marksmanship of riflemen – nicknamed grasshoppers for their dark green uniforms – Wellesley won the Battle of Vimeiro. Then he returned to Westminster to take up his cabinet duties as Secretary for Ireland. But, like Isaac, Wellesley preferred the battlefield to the council room. In the spring of 1809, he accepted command of the British army in Portugal. When he rode through the streets of Coimbra, ladies showered him with roses and sugarplums.

That summer, Isaac moved with his trunk of books from Quebec to Fort George. From here he applied to the governor general, Sir James Craig, for leave to transfer to Portugal. To fight the real fight. Sir James refused the application because, he claimed, he could not spare Isaac. Nor could Upper Canada.

Then, in early autumn, Isaac heard with envy and pride that Wellesley had been made a peer. Though the Battle of Talavera, fought in late July near Madrid, had not been as decisive as Britain would have liked, she rewarded her new darling handsomely. Sir Arthur Wellesley became Viscount Wellington of Talavera. Just as the name of Nelson had once stirred the most jaded of souls, now a new name brought hurrahs. The soldiers of the Peninsular Wars called him Nosey because of his beak; their women called him Our Arthur; but throughout Britain and her colonies the new viscount came to be called Wellington.

∞

Two years later, in June of 1811, Sir James Craig boarded HMS *Amelia*. She was bound for England; he was bound for retirement and death. Isaac was sorry to see him go. True, Sir James was short and fat; true, he had a temper caused by various ailments, including dropsy – but with Isaac he had always been generous and frank. Just before the ailing governor left the Canadas, his adjutant-general, Colonel Edward Baynes, wrote to Isaac that Sir James was sending him a gift. Baynes wrote, "He requests that you will do him the favor to accept as a legacy and mark of his very sincere regard his favorite horse Alfred."

Isaac was touched, and Alfred soon became his own favourite horse. But there were times, typically after a civilian put Isaac in a foul mood, when he could not help looking his gift horse in the mouth. After all, Wellington's favourite charger – he owned seven chargers and seven hunters, and he wore sky blue during foxhunts – was a chestnut mare of fifteen hands named Copenhagen. Isaac's favourite horse – and one did not ride to hounds, not here in the Canadas – was a grey named Alfred.

∞

By the time Ferdinand was writing his memoir of Isaac, historians were analyzing Wellington's victories and trying to pinpoint the decisive moment in each battle. Wellington thought both attempts were futile. "Write the history of a battle?" he scoffed. "As well write the history of a ball." And Isaac, who liked balls – enjoyed the waltz and mazurka – would have agreed. A battle was like a ball, Wellington said, because one remembered one's own partner but little about what other couples were doing. Isaac could have added that the history of a battle, campaign, or war consists not so much of what a soldier knows as of what a soldier does not know. Even a Guernsey Brock.

Or, Ferdinand thought, a Brock Tupper who was trying to reconstruct a famous uncle's life. Clearly, Isaac had had two distinct sides: one official and public, the other personal and private. Sifting through the letters in the box that Savery had kept unopened for thirty years, Ferdinand delighted in the few references to Isaac's personal life. They were like fireflies flashing through the smoke of battle that drifted through every soldier's life. A life of swords and ships and uniforms, which interested Ferdinand no more now than they had in his youth.

He still kept trying to read between the lines. And, now, he watched for the fireflies that could illuminate Isaac's final years. As for Susan Shaw, Ferdinand tried not to think about her.

∽

By early 1811, when Isaac was not travelling in Upper Canada or visiting Quebec, he crisscrossed Lake Ontario by schooner. While at York, he escaped from his tiny cottage in the fort to the houses of William Dummer Powell or Aeneas Shaw, who called his log mansion Oak Hall. While at Fort George, Isaac lived in a pretty cottage with Lieutenant-Colonel John Murray. The previous year, Murray had returned to England to marry. His bride had brought with her not only rose bushes, linens, and plate – both pewter and silver – but also primulas. These were purple Cape primroses sent to her from the Cape of Good Hope by an amateur botanist. Isaac expected that the roses would survive but not the delicate primulas, not here in the wilds of the Canadas.

Isaac and the Murrays had many mutual friends. Among them was Colonel J.A. Vesey, at whose house Isaac had spent a few pleasant days during his leave. The Veseys had six children.

> *Colonel J.A. Vesey to Isaac:*
> Hampton Park Court, April 9, 1811.
> ...I fear you will have passed a lonely winter at Fort George, notwithstanding the addition of my friend Murray and his nice little wife to your society.... I wish I had a daughter old enough for you, as I would give her to you with pleasure. You should be married, particularly as fate seems to detain you so long in Canada – but pray do not marry there.

In early June of 1811, Isaac and Vesey both found themselves promoted to major-general. In Vesey's next letter, he reminded Isaac that a transfer to the Iberian Peninsula could make him what every officer longed to become: a K.B., a Knight of the Order of Bath. Not that Isaac ever admitted to this ambition.

On October 9, 1811, three days after Isaac turned forty-two, the new governor general, Sir George Prevost, named him president and administrator of the government in Upper Canada. The lieutenant governor was home in England on leave. During the year that followed, Isaac's proclamations began like this:

Isaac Brock, Esquire, President, administering the Government of the Province of Upper Canada, and Major-General commanding His Majesty's Forces within the same.
To all whom these Presents shall come, greeting.

And many of his proclamations ended like this:

(Signed) Isaac Brock, President.

The appointment pleased Isaac, but it seemed that the higher he rose, the more he had to hide. Like unexpected – and embarrassing – financial woes.

Isaac to his brother, Irving:
York, October 30, 1811.
My dear friend, – I have at length heard from you. Your letter of the 3d August was only received this day. To what a state of misery are we fallen – poverty I was prepared to bear – but, oh! Irving, if you love me, do not by any action or word add to the sorrows of poor, unfortunate, William....

William had finally persuaded Irving to join him in his business as a merchant. When the firm went bankrupt, partly due to raids by Napoleon's privateers, Irving blamed William.

Soon the creditors found an entry that claimed Isaac owed the firm 3,000 pounds. William had loaned this money privately so that Isaac could buy some of his commissions; but Isaac, as a man of honour, pledged his entire salary as president of the legislature – 1,000 pounds a year – toward discharging his portion of the debt. What pained him more than the blot on his family's good name was the fact that Irving blamed William for the failure. And that Irving, who had always had a way with words, now refused to speak to William.

Isaac spent Wednesday, December 25, 1811 with the Shaw family at Oak Hall, on the outskirts of York. He did not tell Susan of his family's misfortune. She gave him a set of handkerchiefs embroidered with the Brock coat of arms – a lion and a fleur-de-lis below a scallop shell. He gave her, of all things, an oak walking stick with brass fittings and a green wristcord. She pretended it delighted her. Like him, she was becoming good at keeping up pretences.

Colonel Edward Baynes to Isaac:
>   Quebec, January 23, 1812.
> Sir George Prevost has commissioned me to inform you that by the October mail, which arrived two days ago, he received a letter... authorizing him to permit your return to England for the purpose of being employed on the continent, and sanctioning his appointing Major-General Sheaffe to succeed you on the staff in Canada....

Baynes was writing because Sir George wanted confirmation of news he had found incredible, namely that Isaac was now refusing to leave the Canadas for Europe. In a letter dated February 12, Isaac confirmed that this was true. How could he abandon the Canadas even as they were increasingly threatened by invasion?

All of Baynes's letters intrigued Ferdinand because Baynes wrote certain passages in a code that Ferdinand could not break.

∞

Time sped by – one month, then two.

> *Sir George Prevost to Isaac:*
> Quebec, April 30, 1812.
> I have just heard from Mr. Foster that the secretary at war, at Washington, has transmitted orders to Governor Tompkins, of New York, to send 500 of the state militia to Niagara; 500 to the mouth of the Black River, opposite to Kingston; and 600 to Champlain....

Augustus John Foster was the British minister at Washington. Like Isaac, who had done everything he could to prepare for the coming invasion, Foster remained alert. The southern and western states were agitating for war while the northern and eastern states – who stood to lose trade with Britain's colonies – hoped for peace.

But the shrieking of hawks can silence the cooing of doves. On June 18, 1812, the United States declared war on Britain. In secret. The next day, the American president, James Madison, issued a proclamation telling his people they were at war.

The invasion was well underway. Some three weeks before, on June 1, General William Hull had begun marching an army of 2,000 men toward the Black Swamp of northwestern Ohio and into the Michigan Territory. Hull was nearly sixty – a tired hero of the American Revolution who should not have been leading this army, composed of regulars and state militias. They were heading for the Detroit Frontier, along the Detroit River, which flowed south from Lake St. Clair into the northwest corner of Lake Erie. On the American side of the river stood Fort Detroit; on the Canadian side stood the village of Sandwich, where Hull hoped to find sympathizers, of whom – as Isaac well knew – there were many.

∞

Besides letters, proclamations and explanatory narratives, Ferdinand included in his memoir items like newspaper clippings.

From an American newspaper:
Buffalo, July 14, 1812.
Major-General Brock is at present at Newark [Niagara, near Fort George], superintending the various defences on the river. He is stated to be an able and experienced officer, with undoubted courage....

No wonder Uncle Isaac saved this clipping, Ferdinand thought – though, from all that he had heard, Isaac was not a vain man. Perhaps he was simply recording as much as he could of the history of an unreal war.

Ferdinand considered the war unreal for two reasons. First, the real war – the one against Napoleon – was still being fought in Europe. Second, the war in North America was full of intriguing twists and turns. These convinced him that truth – and he did believe that history was true – could be stranger than fiction.

The newspaper clipping continued:

Expecting a descent from the American army, the Canadians have, for ten days past, been removing their families and effects from the river [the Niagara River] into the interior. At Newark, Queenston, and other villages on the river, there are no inhabitants except a few civilians and officers and soldiers. It is even said, that an immense quantity of specie, plate, &c., from various parts of the province, have been boxed up, and destined for Quebec.

So it was that young Mrs. Murray moved from Fort George to York with her linens and her plate. She could not take her roses or primulas, but Isaac and her husband promised that no harm would come to her garden. That they would defend it with their lives.

∽

A proclamation by Brigadier-General William Hull, commanding the North Western Army of the United States:

Head Quarters, Sandwich, July 12, 1812. Inhabitants of Canada! – After thirty years of peace and prosperity, the United States have been driven to arms. The injuries and aggressions, the insults and indignities of Great Britain, have once more left them no alternative but manly resistance or unconditional surrender.

Later in Hull's infamous proclamation, he made a fatal error by saying this:

If the barbarous and savage policy of Great Britain be pursued, and the savages let loose to murder our citizens, and butcher our women and children, this war will be a war of extermination. The first stroke of the tomahawk, the first attempt with the scalping knife, will be the signal of one indiscriminate scene of desolation. No white man, found fighting by the side of an Indian, will be taken prisoner – instant destruction will be his lot.

Hull's error was fatal because it angered Canadian settlers who might otherwise have been sympathetic. If he thought he could summarily execute white men fighting to protect their lands, he needed to learn how civilized men conducted war. And who better to teach Yankee whingers about civility than Canadians?

From a counter-proclamation by Isaac:

Head Quarters, Fort George, July 22, 1812.
Be not dismayed at the unjustifiable threat of
the commander of the enemy's forces to refuse
quarter, should an Indian appear in the ranks. The
brave bands of aborigines which inhabit this
colony were, like his majesty's other subjects, pun-
ished for their zeal and fidelity, by the loss of their
possessions in the late colonies, and rewarded by
his majesty with lands of superior value in this
province....

Like any white man who spoke with a forked
tongue, Isaac said one thing in public and another in
private. Winning the native peoples' support would be
crucial to his repelling the invasion, and yet he trusted
only those natives who supported his cause – those who
despised Americans as fiercely as he did. Imagine, he
had once told Dobson: state militias that elect their
officers!

∞

The unreal war continued.

In early July, after Hull's army had entered the
Michigan Territory, he had arranged for a schooner, the
Cuyahoga, to carry the sick and the army band, his
officers' baggage and his own papers to Fort Detroit.
On the morning of July 2, even as Hull learned that
President Madison had declared war two weeks before,
the *Cuyahoga* was captured while it sailed past Fort
Malden at Amherstburg. The fort and town were in

Upper Canada and close to the mouth of the Detroit River. The schooner was taken by a longboat of Provincial Marines and a canoe of Shawnee warriors, all led by a French-Canadian lieutenant named Charles Frédéric Rolette. While he sailed the *Cuyahoga* into Amherstburg, he made the captured American band play "God Save the King."

Hull's papers made their way to Isaac and, from them, he learned how demoralized Hull and his troops were. And that he was terrified of natives. Isaac liked young Rolette. At twenty-nine, he was a veteran who had been wounded five times. He had fought under Nelson at the Battle of the Nile – as had Captain Sir James Saumarez – and at the Battle of Trafalgar.

Major-General Sir Thomas Saumarez to Isaac:
Halifax, July 22, 1812.
I have great pleasure in having an opportunity to inquire after your health and welfare, and to acquaint you that your relation, Lady Saumarez, and myself, arrived here about a month since....

The American privateers are extremely numerous and daring in this neighbourhood; and, I am sorry to add, they have proved but too successful, having captured several of our vessels bound to Quebec and New Brunswick....

Sir Thomas was the new commandant at Halifax and, like his elder brother, Sir James, Sir Thomas was Isaac's uncle by marriage. It often occurred to Isaac that the war was affecting his entire family – the women as well as the men. For, as Ferdinand tells us here in a footnote, the Lady Saumarez mentioned in this letter was Isaac's first cousin, Harriet Brock.

∽

Seven days later, surprising news reached Quebec.

Isaac to Sir George Prevost:

York, July 29, 1812. I have the honor to transmit herewith a dispatch this instant received from Captain Roberts, announcing the surrender by capitulation, on the 17th instant, of Fort Michilimackinac....

Sir George was stunned. In late June he had written to Charles Roberts to hold his own fort, St. Joseph, against enemy attack. And, if need be, to retreat.

Over 1,100 kilometres by water from York, Fort St. Joseph was the farthest outpost of British military presence in what was then called the Northwest. Some 80 kilometres to the southwest of this fort stood an American outpost, Fort Michilimackinac, on an island in a strait connecting Lake Michigan with Lake Huron.

But in mid-July, Roberts had received a letter from Isaac that contradicted Sir George's orders because Isaac knew that the natives expected the British to be decisive. Hoping that the Americans had not yet heard about the declaration of war, Roberts decided to act. On July 16, he set out with a brig, the *Caledonia*, and with boats and canoes. He led forty-five officers and men of the 10th Royal Veteran Batallion, 180 Canadians, and nearly 400 native warriors. After reaching Michilimackinac early the next morning, the Canadians hauled a six-pound gun onto heights overlooking the fort. At 10:00, Roberts sent the garrison a note suggesting that it surrender before too long. At noon, he hauled down the Stars and Stripes and raised the Union Jack.

The British thus won the first battle of the war – and without firing a shot. While the outcome pleased Sir George, he was furious with Isaac. Isaac wanted to fight an offensive war while Sir George wanted to fight a defensive one. But news and dispatches took a long time to travel in those days, and while this often caused problems, Isaac knew that it could also work in his favour. Especially if he planned to disobey Sir George.

An invented portrait of Tecumseh as if dressed for a European
costume ball. The Shawnee war chief would die in battle
in October of 1813 – one day before his friend, Isaac,
would have turned forty-four.

8

The Saviour of Upper Canada

T ime sped by – one week, then two.

Just before midnight on Thursday, August 13,
Isaac reached Amherstburg. Militiamen and civilians,
lit by torches, cheered his arrival. Even as he clam-
bered onto the wharf, 500 Shawnee, including a war
chief named Tecumseh, fired their muskets into the air.
Isaac told the local Indian agent to stop the firing to
save ammunition. This impressed Tecumseh, who was
prepared to dislike Isaac for being just another soldier
turned governor. They met in the early hours of Friday
morning at Fort Malden. Using his scalping knife to
score the back of a piece of bark, Tecumseh sketched

the terrain near Fort Detroit. Isaac nodded, equally impressed, while Tecumseh described how his warriors had kept harassing Hull's columns and patrols.

Shortly after Hull had reached Fort Detroit, Isaac had sent a Colonel Henry Proctor to take command of men of the 41st stationed at Fort Malden. Now, during councils of war, Isaac saw that Tecumseh did not trust Proctor, who could not hide his low opinion of natives; but, as Isaac knew from his dealings with Roger Sheaffe, a commander could not always choose his senior officers. Tecumseh seemed to know this, as well.

Isaac had arrived at Amherstburg with volunteers from the York and Norfolk militias, more regulars of the 41st Foot, and Iroquois warriors. At his side were two aides-de-camp: Captain John B. Glegg of the 49th and Lieutenant-Colonel John Macdonell. Many years later, Glegg gave the following description to Ferdinand, who was still trying to understand what Isaac and the Shawnee war chief might have had in common:

> "...Tecumseh's appearance was very prepossessing; his figure light and finely proportioned; his age I imagined to be about five and thirty; in height, five feet nine or ten inches; his complexion, light copper; countenance, oval, with bright hazel eyes, beaming cheerfulness, energy, and decision...."

Ferdinand's footnote:
His age was then about forty.

Tecumseh meant "the Panther Passing Across." Even as he was born on a Wednesday in March, a year and a half before Isaac, a meteor called the Panther crossed the night sky from north to south. The Panther was searching for its lair, and the sky blazed greenish-white in the Panther's silent wake.

∞

Under a flag of truce, Captain Glegg crossed the Detroit River.

Isaac to Brigadier-General William Hull:
Head Quarters, Sandwich, Aug. 15, 1812. The force at my disposal authorizes me to require of you the immediate surrender of Fort Detroit. It is far from my inclination to join in a war of extermination; but you must be aware that the numerous body of Indians who have attached themselves to my troops, will be beyond my control the moment the contest commences.

Isaac had learned well by watching Nelson seal his ultimatum at the Battle of Copenhagen. The Danish Crown Prince had surrendered because he had thought that Nelson would, indeed, set fire to all the floating batteries he had supposedly captured. Isaac knew that Hull's troops outnumbered his own by two to one, but Isaac also knew what – that is to say, whom – Hull most feared.

Glegg returned with a terse reply that was full of bravado.

Brigadier-General William Hull to Isaac:
Head Quarters, Detroit, Aug. 15, 1812.
I have received your letter of this date. I have
no other reply to make than to inform you, that I
am prepared to meet any force which may be at
your disposal, and any consequences which may
result from any exertion of it you may think
proper to make.
(Signed) W. Hull, Brigadier-General,
Commanding the N.W. Army of the U.S.

Isaac scowled. Then he recalled the reply from
the Comte de Frontenac to Sir William Phips: that
Frontenac had no answer but what he could give with
the mouths of his cannon. But Hull was no Frontenac,
and Fort Detroit was no Quebec.

Against the advice of most of his officers, Isaac
crossed to the American side of the river. During the
afternoon, he watched while British guns fired on the
fort and American guns answered; then he ordered the
British guns to cease fire. He returned to the Canadian
side of the river. That night, the local Indian agent and
600 native warriors – most of them Shawnee – crossed
the river. At 6:00 on Sunday, August 16, Isaac led a
small flotilla across the river while the sun rose and
British guns fired on Fort Detroit. With him, in boats
and canoes, were 300 regulars, 400 militia, and five
light guns.

And here Isaac was bluffing again. He had
ordered the militia dressed in old uniforms of the 41st
Foot so that Hull would think most of the militiamen
were regulars.

Yet Tecumseh went one better. Knowing that all natives looked alike to white men, he led his warriors in single file in front of a wood on the far side of a field – in full view of the Americans. Then the warriors slipped behind the trees, ran back to the starting point, and once again filed in front of the wood. After the warriors had done this twice, the Americans thought Tecumseh had three times as many men as he really had.

Or so this story goes. No wonder Isaac and Tecumseh became such fast friends that they gave one another the sashes they wore. Isaac gave Tecumseh a scarlet general's sash. Tecumseh gave Isaac a sash with fringed ends and a pattern of lightning bolts. They were cut from the same cloth: Master Isaac and the Panther Passing Across.

Surprising news reached Quebec once more.

Isaac to Sir George Prevost:
Head Quarters, Detroit, Aug. 16, 1812.
I hasten to apprize your excellency of the capture of this very important post: 2,500 troops have this day surrendered prisoners of war, and about 25 pieces of ordnance have been taken without the sacrifice of a drop of British blood. I had not more than 700 troops, including militia, and about 600 Indians, to accomplish this service. When I detail my good fortune, your excellency will be astonished….

Sir George was beside himself with fury, but what could he do – with Isaac now the man of the hour? Sir George wrote to Lord Bathurst, the secretary for war in London, about this second – and even more surprising – victory.

As for Hull, he was imprisoned at Montreal and, after his release, became a scapegoat for the War Hawks. He was court-martialled for losing Fort Detroit and the Michigan Territory and condemned to death by firing squad. In light of Hull's service during the American Revolution, President Madison commuted the sentence. Had the strange new rumour begun spreading at once, Madison might not have been so lenient.

According to this rumour, the battle for Fort Detroit was a sham. With his men sick and his chief medical officer dead, Hull wanted to surrender, and so he wrote to Isaac and proposed that the Americans merely pretend to offer resistance. After both sides exchanged cannon fire, Isaac could cross the river and accept Hull's sword. Isaac apparently agreed. Yet no one could confirm this rumour because, if Isaac and Hull did trade such damning letters, both men destroyed the evidence.

∽

Isaac to his brothers:

Head Quarters, Detroit, Aug. 16, 1812.

My dear Brothers and Friends, – Rejoice at my good fortune, and join me in prayers to Heaven. I send you a copy of my hasty note to Sir George.

Let me hear that you are all *united* and happy.

Ferdinand's footnote:
This letter, addressed to his brother Irving in London, reached him, we believe, on the 13th of October, the very day on which the writer was slain.

Here, again, time was behaving strangely – now because of the sheer amount of time it took for news to cross the Atlantic: as much as two months. And so, to everyone in Britain – Isaac's brothers and sisters, the Prince Regent himself – Isaac would remain alive for some weeks after his death on Queenston Heights.

Early on the morning of Tuesday, October 6, while Sally and William strolled in a park, guns began to boom and church bells ring out. Sally looked to William for an explanation. "For Isaac, of course," William teased. "Do you not know that this is his birthday?" After they returned home, their one remaining servant said that great news had reached London – as had the colours of an American regiment captured in mid-August. A dispatch from Master Isaac was, even now, being printed in a *Gazette Extraordinary.* People were calling him the Saviour of Upper Canada.

Lord Bathurst to Sir George Prevost:
Downing Street, October 10, 1812.
I have had the honor of receiving your dispatch, dated the 26th of August, together with its

enclosures, from Major-General Brock, and I lost no time in laying intelligence so important and satisfactory before his royal highness the prince regent.

Ferdinand's footnote:
"Whitehall, October 10, 1812. – His royal highness the prince regent has been pleased, in the name and on the behalf of his majesty, to nominate and appoint Major-General Isaac Brock to be an Extra Knight of the Most Honorable Order of the Bath."

Two months later, the Prince Regent told a friend that, if Isaac had survived the Battle of Queenston Heights, the Prince Regent would have made him a baronet and awarded him a pension of 1,200 pounds a year. Imagine that, Ferdinand thought. Isaac's new proclamations could have ended like this:

(Signed) Sir Isaac Brock, K.B., Bart.

∞

Time continued behaving strangely. Letters like the next one reached Britain even as families named Brock, Tupper, and De Lisle steeled themselves for yet another sad Christmas.

Isaac to his brothers:
Lake Ontario, Sept. 3, 1812.
It is supposed that the value of the articles captured will amount to 30 or £40,000; in that

case, my proportion will be something consider-able. If it enable me to contribute to your comfort and happiness, I shall esteem it my highest reward…. The want of union was nearly losing this province without even a struggle, and be assured it operates in the same degree in regard to families.

Even if the prize money could help William and Irving repay some of their creditors, there was still the brothers' estrangement – which, as irony piled upon coincidence, ended on Tuesday, October 13. The day of Isaac's last charge.

That morning, seeing Irving in the financial dis-trict, William went up to him and the brothers shook hands. Then Irving showed William a brief letter he had just received from Isaac – the letter that ended, "Let me hear that you are all *united* and happy." Irving had decided to send this letter to William as a way of apologizing for his own stubborn silence.

ᄋᄋ

The unreal war continued and time sped by – four weeks, then six.

Isaac to his brother, Savery:
Fort George, September 18, 1812.
…You will hear of some decided action in the course of a fortnight, or in all probability we shall return to a state of tranquility. I say decisive, because if I should be beaten, the province is inevitably gone; and should I be victorious, I do

not imagine the gentry from the other side will be anxious to return to the charge....

After the fall of Fort Detroit, Isaac had found himself increasingly annoyed with Sir George. In early August, Sir George had signed an armistice with the American commander-in-chief; but Isaac did not hear about this till a week after he captured Fort Detroit. Worse yet, at the end of August, Sir George issued a general order in which he all but apologized for Isaac's having invaded American territory. It was Isaac's turn to be stunned.

By early September, word arrived that President Madison had refused to accept the armistice. Why would he? The Americans had used the lull to move more troops across New York State. The next invasion would occur somewhere along the Niagara Frontier, Isaac knew, but where? From Buffalo and Black Rock across to Fort Erie, where Lake Erie squeezed itself into the Niagara River? From Lewiston across to Queenston? Impossible. The Americans would lose half their men to the fast-flowing river if they tried to cross here, only ten kilometres below Niagara Falls. The most likely crossing, he thought, would be from Youngstown to Fort George, where the river joined Lake Ontario. And so he based himself once again at the Murrays' pretty cottage.

Isaac had forgotten what he had once told FitzGibbon: that the word *impossible* should not be found in a soldier's dictionary. But Isaac was dead tired. He slept three or four hours a night and was so highly strung that he lost his temper daily. He shrugged this off. After winning the war, he could return to his former cheery self. There would be dancing again.

∞

Isaac knew that the war had to be won on water as well as on land. Although he scoffed at the lack of discipline shown by the enemy soldiers, especially by militiamen, he had a grudging respect for the sailors and marines.

Isaac to Sir George Prevost:
> Fort George, October 11, 1812. The enemy is making every exertion to gain a naval superiority on both lakes, which if they accomplish I do not see how we can retain the country. More vessels are fitting out for war on the other side of Squaw Island, which I should have attempted to destroy but for your excellency's repeated instructions to forbear....

For weeks, Isaac had kept suggesting that he also capture Sacket's Harbor, New York, but Sir George had kept demurring.

Sacket's Harbor stood at the mouth of Black River Bay at the eastern end of Lake Ontario some fifty-six kilometres southeast of Kingston. During the armistice, the Americans had massed schooners and boats as a first step toward ending British control of the Great Lakes. Isaac did not know how many vessels he could capture – only that he had to keep taking the fight to the enemy.

Then, in early October, the British lost two vessels on Lake Erie. One was a schooner, the *Caledonia*; the other was a brig, the *Adams*. She had been in drydock for repairs when Hull had surrendered. Isaac had renamed her the *Detroit* and placed young Lieutenant Rolette in command. The loss troubled Colonel Henry Proctor, at Amherstburg, where supplies of food were dwindling – as they were in other parts of the colony.

∞

Ferdinand found two final letters from Isaac. He had addressed the first to Colonel Proctor, but because it bore no date, Ferdinand decided that it may not have been sent. In it Isaac mentioned that Wellington had defeated Marmont, a French marshall, near Salamanca. Isaac added, "I consider the game nearly up in Spain."

> *Ferdinand's footnote:*
> "It is also creditable to the military character of the little island of Guernsey, that of the five British generals killed in action in 1812, two... were Major-General Le Marchant, 6th Dragoon Guards, at the battle of Salamanca, and Major-General Sir Isaac Brock, K.B., 49th Foot, in America." – *Duncan's History of Guernsey.*

Whether a Brock, a Saumarez, or a Le Marchant, they were all at war now. As for the second letter, Ferdinand decided that this was likely the last time Isaac touched paper, pen, and ink.

Isaac to Sir George Prevost:

October 12, 1812. The vast number of troops which have been this day added to the strong force previously collected on the opposite side, convinces me, with other indications, that an attack is not far distant. I have in consequence directed every exertion to be made to complete the militia to 2,000 men, but fear that I shall not be able to effect my object with willing, well-disposed characters. Were it not for the numbers of Americans in our ranks, we might defy all their efforts against this part of the province.

∽

On the evening of Monday, October 12, Isaac went to bed late, as usual – well past midnight, which made it early on Tuesday, October 13.

Too tired to sleep, he wondered how much one man could be expected to do. In these past few weeks he had tried to do so much that he could not remember all that he had planned. And when. Or all that he had accomplished. If anything. Then he decided he was not one man; he was many men. He was all his brothers and his brothers in arms and, if they had to, they would link those arms from Fort George through Queenston to Fort Erie, and God help the filthy rabble that tried to break through.

Moments later, it seemed, he awoke.

He could hear thunder coming from the south, but the falls were too far away for even their booming to carry like this. Cannon fire at Queenston. Isaac began to dress. After pulling on his breeches, he reached for the coat he had worn as a brigadier. The ride would be muddy, and there was little time for show. Still, after buttoning the lapels to his throat, he tied around his waist his new sash with its pattern of lightning bolts.

He wondered about Thomas Evans's report. Earlier on Monday, Evans, the brigade major at Fort George, had crossed from Queenston to Lewiston to deliver a message to the Americans. He had seen a number of boats hidden behind bushes along the shore. By evening he had returned to Fort George and reported his findings to Isaac, who had ordered the militia put on alert.

Isaac pulled on his boots and buckled on his sword. Then he jammed his cocked hat onto his head, snatched up his pocket watch and telescope, and marched outside. A soldier had saddled Alfred and held his reins. Macdonell and Glegg were awaiting orders. They had not believed Evans's claim that the Americans would cross from Lewiston. Nor had Isaac. Even now he was sure this attack on Queenston was a diversion from the impending attack on Fort George. And so, even as he climbed into the saddle, he told his aides to tell Sheaffe to keep most of the troops here.

Then Isaac was off, headed south past Brown's Point and Vrooman's Point to Queenston.

It was raining heavily. Wiping the rain from his face, he realized he had forgotten his handkerchief. What did this matter now? He would be soaked by the end of the ride. Muddy and wet like Alfred, who was trying to outrace the wind. And while Isaac rode, at times bent toward Alfred's mane, he thought of other rides – up Mount Hillaby in green and lush Barbados – and he laughed at the galloping excitement of the chase.

This was how he would feel one day – riding to the hounds in Spain. But he would not wear sky blue. He liked the colour of this sky. It was grey and black and full of clouds; yet the clouds no longer looked like castles or knights or ships. All his life he had looked for images and patterns. He had found them where there should have been none. He had made whatever sense of them he could. Wondering where he might be spending Christmas this year, he found himself lying on damp leaves and willing the clouds to part. A boy wept nearby. Isaac looked at the suns or the fireflies or the faces of the two lovely women, both of them smiling now. Reached up to touch the stars.

The present Brock Monument's inauguration in 1859 – some years after a supporter of the 1837 Rebellion nearly demolished an earlier Brock Monument with a gunpowder blast.

Epilogue

One Last Climb

O n the first Monday in July of 1867, an old woman sat with her back to a limestone monument and watched the sun rise over Queenston Heights. She was trying to remember her age. Seventy-seven seemed about right. That meant he would have turned... ninety-eight this year.

Nodding, she cupped her left hand over the yellowing ivory knob of her walking stick. It was made of oak. Below the knob, a pattern of rings belled in and out and, below this, the ferrule joining the handle to the shaft was brass. An unravelling green wristcord passed through the shaft. The oval eyelets and the finial were brass, as well. Yet it was the pattern that delighted her; that she caressed with the papery finger-tips of her right hand. What an odd present it had been – the same Christmas she had given him the set of embroidered handkerchiefs. Many years later, alone in her lamplit room, she had finally discovered the secret of this walking stick. Now, only she knew.

She breathed in air that was already too warm. Other years, she came to mark his birthday, when maples blazed and frost hardened like whitecaps on the waves of muddy roads. But today there had been no whitecaps on the lake during her crossing by steamer from Toronto. Such an odd name, not like York. She had arrived the previous afternoon with two young people whose last name was…Baldwin. They were still asleep at Mr. Wynn's Hotel in the village. She could not decide whether they were a nephew and niece or the children of a nephew. But she knew that they were eager to return to Toronto because, this afternoon, there would be outdoor concerts and, tonight, fire-works. All this fuss to celebrate the birth of a country called the Dominion of Canada.

As for the young peoples' Christian names, she could not remember these from one week to the next and so, today, she thought of them as George and Caroline. She liked them both even if she did find George's ideas far too progressive. Still, he and his sis-ter were kind to her in spite of her forgetfulness; in spite of her spinning what they considered fairy tales. And so, no matter what she called George and Caroline, they addressed her politely as Aunt Susan.

Chuckling, she rearranged the skirts of her long black dress. Then she turned as if to share the joke with the man who would have turned ninety-eight this year, but she stopped herself. The monument was spectacular, but she did not need to look at it to know that he was there. In the limestone. Waiting for her. She would rather look at the rising sun. At the way its rays bent around the rings on the walking stick when she held it in front of any bright light. When she squinted just so and –

No, she did not need to look. She knew he was there.

Behind her – beyond the dwarf wall with the sculpted military trophies at each corner – a door led to a corridor, which led to the tombs and the stairs. In one tomb were Isaac's remains. In the other were those of John Macdonell. Poor Mary Powell. She had been inconsolable when they had learned that he had joined Isaac in death. As had Alfred, that fine, grey horse. But how many people grieved for a horse? And the other dead – she could not remember all their names. Only that Roger Sheaffe had boasted of having won the battle when everyone had known it had been the natives. For the natives had terrified the Americans into throwing themselves off the heights into the river below. Or gladly surrendering. George, her nephew or her nephew's son, insisted that the hidden story of the war was the story of men like Tecumseh, but who would believe such a fairy tale? Everyone believed, as they should, that Isaac had won the war if not the battle. That he had laid the foundations for this new dominion by uniting its people in a common cause.

Her heart began to race, as it did whenever she thought of Americans. This was why, most of the time, she tried not to think of them at all. Tried to think, instead, of walks in apple orchards, of waltzes and mazurkas, and of his manly profile. She chuckled once more while she lowered the walking stick. Proof, they had all said after the war. What proof do you have? Anyone could have written those letters you claim to have burned. But the proof would go with her to the grave, and –

No, she had never been inside, yet she could see the morning light piercing the openings carved like wreaths. Nor had she ever climbed the stairs, all those steps that rose through the pedestal with its bas-relief of the battle; up through the cap with more wreathed openings; up through the fluted shaft of the pillar; up to the capital with its four winged Victories; and finally into the round chamber with its wreathed portals – from which climbers could gaze on lush farmlands or across the Niagara into enemy territory.

They would always be the enemy. One day the Americans would come again, but next time there would be no Isaac Brock to save this new Dominion of Canada. Not that anyone believed her when she said they would come again. These days, the Americans were licking their wounds, and not just from the war. From yet another war of their own making: a civil war in which brother killed brother and sister betrayed sister. But what could one expect from such filthy, rebellious rabble? As Isaac's mother had called them once. Rightly so, and –

Oh, those perfidious Brocks. She never spoke ill of them, but she would never forgive them. Ever.

First she had written to his sister, Elizabeth, and introduced herself. "Though this does not mean I seek any favour from you and yours," she had written. Elizabeth Brock Tupper of St. Peter Port, Guernsey, did not bother to reply. Years later, when Ferdinand's memoir appeared, Susan ordered it from London – both editions – and it made her weep. Not one mention of her, but did he have to include that hurtful letter from a supposed friend? The letter that ended, "Pray do not marry there." And so she wrote to Ferdinand Brock Tupper, Esq., of St. Peter Port, but he did not reply. Nor did William Brock, Esq., of London, to whom the Duke of York had sent a medal from the Prince Regent himself.

She had never held it, but she knew its every detail: large, gold, and made to be worn about the neck. On the obverse, Britannia in her splendour; on the reverse, "Detroit"; and, around the rim, "Major-General Sir Isaac Brock." Poor Isaac. How could he have known, even as he had charged up these heights, that he could have worn the star of the Order of Bath? The one he had so admired on Nelson's breast. But Nelson could not boast of a monument as magnificent as this. Nor could Wellington, and he had become a duke and then a prime minister, and at his funeral –

No, she had never climbed the steps even when she had been young. She could not bear the thought of standing in the round chamber while Isaac rose, three times larger than life, beyond her reach. While he bore on his shoulders the weight of the sky.

How she had loved those shoulders. How she had laughed when she had stood on tiptoes, linked her arms about his neck, and pulled his face down to kiss hers. Then, with his arms wrapped around her waist, he would lift her off her feet and twirl her like a child. Like the child he claimed she was – but only because he was nearly twice her age that last Christmas they had spent together at Oak Hall. The Christmas he had given her this. She raised the walking stick again and shook it at the sun. Proof, is it? she heard herself shout. Here's my proof:

He sleeps beside me every night. Take even this from me, if you can. This very walking stick that supports and comforts me.

For, each night before she went to bed, she would steady the handle in front of a lamp and smile at him in welcome. When George and Caroline looked at the handle, all they saw were the yellowing ivory knob and, above the brass ferrule, the carved rings belling in and out. But when Susan held it in front of a lamp – the way she held it now, once again, in front of the sun – the lamp cast Isaac's profile on her wall. There he was with his leonine head, his broad brow, and his strong chin. The rest, she could add, the way a child adds colour to a silhouette: the blue-grey eyes, the fair hair, the pink tinge of his lips. There he was each night in her room as he would be for all eternity – here on Queenston Heights, and beside her, in her grave:

Master Isaac.

Her beloved Isaac.

Larger than life.

Early in the Battle of Queenston Heights, by the artistic
Captain James Dennis. Isaac will soon gallop through Queenston
on his favourite horse, Alfred – both of them doomed.

Chronology of Isaac Brock (1769-1812)

Compiled by Lynne Bowen

BROCK AND HIS TIMES	THE CANADAS AND THE WORLD
	1728 James Cook, future maritime explorer, is born in Yorkshire. He is the son of an agricultural day labourer.
1729 John Brock (Brock's father) is born; he will serve in his youth as a midshipman in the Royal Navy.	**1729** Britain takes possession of Gibraltar following the Anglo-Spanish War.
	1750 In New France, French fur traders build Fort Rouillé at the entry to the Toronto Passage, a shortcut overland between Lakes Ontario and Huron.
	1755 Anticipating the British war with France, James Cook joins the Royal Navy as an able seaman.

BROCK AND HIS TIMES

THE CANADAS AND THE WORLD

1756
In Europe, the Seven Years' War begins; Prussia and Britain are allies against almost every other European state; Britain is intent on seizing French colonies.

British privateers are licensed by the government to sail from the colonial ports of Halifax, Liverpool, Shelburne, Annapolis Royal, St. Andrews, and Saint John and capture and pillage the ships of Britain's enemies.

1758
John Brock marries Elizabeth De Lisle; they will have fourteen children, ten of whom will survive infancy.

1758
In England, Horatio Nelson (future British naval hero) is born at Burnham Thorpe in Norfolk.

James Cook, as master of the *Pembroke,* is at the siege of Louisbourg, Ile Royale (Cape Breton Island).

1759
John Brock (Brock's eldest brother) is born.

1759
In the waters off New France, James Cook charts the navigable channel up the St. Lawrence River; this enables British general James Wolfe to bring his ships to Quebec City where he leads his troops in the defeat of French troops led by the Marquis de Montcalm at the Battle of the Plains of Abraham; both generals die; Fort Rouillé (Toronto) is burned by its retreating French garrison.

BROCK AND HIS TIMES	THE CANADAS AND THE WORLD

1760
Ferdinand Brock (Brock's second eldest brother) is born.

1760
In New France, Montreal surrenders to the British.

In Britain, George II dies; his grandson George III (Farmer George) succeeds him.

1762
Daniel De Lisle Brock (Brock's third eldest brother) is born.

1763
The Treaty of Paris ends the Seven Years' War; Britain assumes control of New France and emerges as the world leader in overseas colonial enterprise. The Royal Proclamation of King George III establishes a framework for negotiation of Indian treaties and becomes one of several matters which anger his subjects to the south of New France in the Thirteen Colonies, where the conflict has been called the French and Indian War.

James Cook begins a four-year-long project to chart the coast of Newfoundland.

c. 1765
Elizabeth Brock (Brock's eldest sister) is born.

1766
William Brock (Brock's paternal grandfather) dies.

BROCK AND HIS TIMES

THE CANADAS AND THE WORLD

1768
Tecumseh or The Panther Passing Across (future Shawnee war chief) is born in what will become the American state of Ohio.

Because of his charting abilities, James Cook is made an officer and given command of HMS *Endeavour*; he embarks on a three-year-long voyage around the world and becomes the first Englishman to find New Zealand and Australia.

1769
Isaac Brock is born on October 6 in St. Peter Port, Guernsey (Channel Islands); he is the eighth son of John and Elizabeth De Lisle Brock.

1769
Arthur Wellesley (future Duke of Wellington) is born in Dublin, Ireland.

Napoleone Buonaparte (future Emperor of France) is born on Corsica, an island in the Mediterranean Sea recently acquired by France.

1770
Horatio Nelson goes to sea at the age of twelve.

1772
James Cook leaves on a second three-year-long circumnavigation of the globe; William Bligh and George Vancouver are members of the crew.

1773
Savery Brock (Brock's favourite younger brother) is born.

BROCK AND HIS TIMES	THE CANADAS AND THE WORLD
	1774 The Quebec Act is passed in Britain; it establishes the Province of Quebec which includes present-day Ontario and extends south into the Ohio Valley; Americans are outraged that Quebec has acquired Indian territory as a result of the act and consider it another of the "intolerable acts" which will cause the American Revolution.
1775 Brock begins his schooling at Elizabeth College on the island of Guernsey.	**1775** In April, the American War of Independence begins; American forces take possession of Montreal and attack Quebec City; American privateers harass every outpost in Nova Scotia outside Halifax.
	1776 In Quebec, American soldiers abandon Montreal in May; the Thirteen Colonies declare their independence from Britain on July 4.

James Cook begins a voyage to search for the Northwest Passage from Bering Strait on the west side. |
| **1777** John Brock dies while taking the waters in Brittany and leaves ten fatherless children. | **1777** In the wake of American victories over British forces, France recognizes the Thirteen Colonies as a nation. |
| | **1778** An American mob lynches a Shawnee chief; the Shawnee enter the American War of Independence on the British side. |

BROCK AND HIS TIMES

THE CANADAS AND THE WORLD

James Cook anchors in Nootka Sound on Vancouver Island.

1779
Battling strong tides, ten-year-old Brock swims 800 metres to Castle Cornet and then back; he goes to school in Southampton on the south coast of England.

Ferdinand Brock dies in the Battle of Baton Rouge in September; the news doesn't reach Guernsey until late in the year.

1779
Spain declares war on Britain in order to help the Thirteen Colonies; Spain captures Baton Rouge, a British possession.

In Nova Scotia, the British clear the Bay of Fundy of American privateers.

In France, Napoleone Buonaparte enters a military academy in Brienne.

William Dummer Powell comes from Britain to Montreal to practise law; he becomes a spokesperson for Loyalist dissatisfaction with the Quebec Act.

James Cook is murdered in the Sandwich Islands (Hawaii).

1781
British forces surrender to rebel Americans in October.

1782
In North America, fourteen-year-old Tecumseh sees battle for the first time; he runs away in fright.

1783
In North America, Tecumseh sees battle for the second time; he kills four white men but denounces death by torture and convinces his fellow Shawnee to do the same.

| BROCK AND HIS TIMES | THE CANADAS AND THE WORLD |

THE CANADAS AND THE WORLD

The Treaty of Paris formally recognizes the United States of America (U.S.); a flood of colonists loyal to the British Crown (Loyalists) leave the U.S. and move into Nova Scotia and Quebec, where they settle in quickly surveyed townships along the St. Lawrence River, around Kingston, and in the Niagara Peninsula; field officers from disbanded military units get the largest pieces of land.

1784
After Brock finishes school in Southampton, his mother sends him to Rotterdam for a year to learn proper French from a Protestant minister.

1784
Napoleone Buonaparte is selected to attend the *École Militaire* in Paris.

1785
Brock buys a commission as an ensign in the 8th (the King's) Regiment of the British army; his brother, John, is a captain in the same regiment.

1785
Napoleone Buonaparte graduates from military college and is commissioned as a second lieutenant of artillery in the French army.

1787
Arthur Wellesley enters the British army; he becomes aide-de-camp to the Lord Lieutenant of Ireland.

1788
King George III of Britain suffers the first in a series of episodes of insanity.

1789
Avenging the deaths of his father and brother, Techumseh fights the

BROCK AND HIS TIMES	THE CANADAS AND THE WORLD
	American army in a series of battles.
	The fall of the Bastille marks the symbolic beginning of the French Revolution.
	The crew of HMS *Bounty* mutiny against their captain, William Bligh.
1790 Brock buys a commission as a lieutenant; he is quartered on the Channel Islands.	
1791 Brock is promoted to captain; he changes regiments to the 49th Foot so he can be posted abroad; he is sent to Barbados; he wins a duel.	**1791** The Constitution Act divides the old Province of Quebec into Lower and Upper Canada along the present-day Quebec-Ontario border.
Savery Brock signs a petition condemning the mastheading of midshipmen; he resigns from the Royal Navy and joins the army.	William Bligh takes command of HMS *Providence*.
Brock's personal servant, Dobson, joins him.	
1792 Brock is posted to Kingston, Jamaica; Dobson nurses him through a serious illness, probably yellow fever.	**1792** France deposes King Louis XVI to make way for the First French Republic.
	Captain George Vancouver spends the first of three summers heading a maritime expedition to explore the west coast of North America from California to Alaska.

BROCK AND HIS TIMES	**THE CANADAS AND THE WORLD**
1793 Brock returns to Guernsey to recuperate; he is then posted to the British army recruiting service in England and Jersey.	**1793** Arthur Wellesley acquires the rank of lieutenant-colonel in the British army partly by favour and partly by purchase.
	In Upper Canada, Governor Simcoe orders a small town to be laid out at the site of Fort Rouillé and names it York.
	In France, Napoleone Buonaparte is promoted to brigadier-general; the Reign of Terror begins; in the next year 20,000 French people including King Louis and Queen Marie Antoinette are beheaded.
	1794 In the Netherlands, Arthur Wellesley serves in the Duke of York's unsuccessful campaign.
	In Upper Canada, William Dummer Powell becomes a judge of the Court of King's Bench; Governor Simcoe names York the capital.
1795 Brock buys a major's commission; his mother, Elizabeth, dies.	**1795** General Napoleone Buonaparte quells an uprising of malcontents in Paris and places himself in the good graces of the Directory, as the current French government is called; he adopts the French spelling of his name: Napoléon Bonaparte.

BROCK AND HIS TIMES

THE CANADAS AND THE WORLD

1796
Arthur Wellesley goes to India to serve in the army; his brother is India's governor general.

In Upper Canada, parliament buildings are erected at York; Fort George is established on the west side of the Niagara River and will serve as the headquarters for the British Indian Department in Upper Canada.

Napoléon Bonaparte marries Joséphine de Beauharnais; his victorious "Italian" campaign begins.

1797
Brock buys a lieutenant-colonel's commission and soon becomes commander of the 49th Regiment; he transforms the regiment from one of the worst in the British army to one of the best; Roger Hale Sheaffe is his second-in-command.

1797
At the Battle of Tenerife, Horatio Nelson, having already lost the sight in his right eye in Corsica, loses his right arm.

1798
Horatio Nelson wins a barony for his victory over Napoléon Bonaparte in Aboukir Bay near the mouth of the Nile in Egypt; he sails to Naples where he meets Emma, Lady Hamilton; their ensuing romance disrupts his marriage.

George Vancouver publishes his journals in which he claims to have proven the existence of a north-

BROCK AND HIS TIMES	THE CANADAS AND THE WORLD

THE CANADAS AND THE WORLD

west passage connecting the Atlantic and Pacific oceans.

1799
Brock's regiment goes to Holland where a joint British/Russian force tries to restore the Dutch monarchy; Brock leads the regiment into battle at Egmont-op-Zee; he is wounded but is saved by the cotton handkerchief he wears over his cravat; Sergeant James FitzGibbon joins the 49th Regiment and is captured by the French and held prisoner for three months.

1799
Britain and Russia invade the Netherlands in the hope that the Dutch will rise up against their French conquerors; the invasion is unsuccessful.

Napoléon Bonaparte becomes First Consul in France, he creates a highly centralized government; he supervises the creation of a code of customs and laws (the Napoleonic Code) which includes the subjugation of women and the restoration of slavery in the colonies.

1801
Brock sails toward the Baltic Sea aboard HMS *Ganges* with a huge fleet; Vice-Admiral Nelson commands one squadron; Brock watches the Battle of Copenhagen and sees Nelson use a written ultimatum to effect Denmark's surrender.

Brock's brother, John, dies at Cape of Good Hope in a duel.

1801
For his destruction of the Danish navy off Copenhagen, Horatio Nelson is made a viscount.

France concludes a peace treaty with Austria.

William Bligh and John Franklin are among the Royal Navy officers taking part in the bombardment of Copenhagen.

1802
In the spring, Brock goes to Upper Canada with his regiment for garrison duty; enroute he meets James FitzGibbon, who impresses him with his eagerness to learn; Brock promotes FitzGibbon to sergeant major.

1802
Arthur Wellesley is promoted to major-general.

France concludes a peace treaty with Britain; Napoléon is made consul for life and drops the name "Bonaparte." To the English-

BROCK AND HIS TIMES	THE CANADAS AND THE WORLD
	speaking world he becomes known simply as "Napoleon."

BROCK AND HIS TIMES

1803
Stationed at York in Upper Canada, Brock and his men take after deserters by rowing at night across Lake Ontario to Fort George near Niagara.

Brock with FitzGibbon arrests a group of mutineers, who are sentenced to be executed; some of the deserters are transported to the West Indies.

1804
Executions of mutineers and deserters, which take place in Quebec in March, are badly botched; Brock receives a detailed report in York; a grief-stricken Brock informs the men of his regiment.

1805
Brock is promoted to full colonel; he goes home on leave, which he spends in Guernsey with his sister Elizabeth Brock Tupper, and in England with his brother William and sister-in-law Sally in London and his sister Mary Potenger in Compton, Berkshire; he confers with the Duke of York, commander-in-chief of the army, regarding the defence of Upper and Lower Canada against the Americans.

THE CANADAS AND THE WORLD

1803
War between France and Britain is rekindled; Lord Nelson is made commander-in-chief, Mediterranean, and patrols the south coast of France on HMS *Victory*; Napoleon prepares to invade England.

1804
In the presence of Pope Pius VII, Napoleon crowns himself Emperor of the French.

1805
Near the Strait of Gibraltar Lord Nelson engages the French and Spanish fleets at the Battle of Trafalgar; the British are triumphant but Nelson dies of his wounds.

Arthur Wellesley returns from India to England; he is knighted and elected a member of the British House of Commons.

In the Battle of Austerlitz, Napoleon defeats Austria and Russia.

BROCK AND HIS TIMES

1806
Brock cuts his leave short when news from Europe and North America alarms him; he leaves Guernsey for the last time and sails back to North America on the *Lady Saumarez*.

1807
Brock worries needlessly about the loyalty of Lower Canada; he is promoted to brigadier-general by Sir James Craig, the new governor general.

1808
Savery Brock serves as an aide-de-camp in the Peninsular Wars in Spain.

1809
After Brigadier-General Baron de Rottenberg arrives in Lower Canada, Brock is ordered back to Upper Canada; he moves from Quebec to Fort George where he applies to Craig for leave to trans-

THE CANADAS AND THE WORLD

1806
In England, Arthur Wellesley marries Kitty Pakenham, daughter of the Earl of Longford.

After defeating Austria, Prussia, and Russia, Napoleon controls most of Europe and his brothers sit on three European thrones; he imposes a continental blockade against British trade, but Britain still controls the seas; this enrages the Americans, who are looking for an excuse to invade the Canadas.

1807
Sir James Craig becomes governor general and commander-in-chief in British North America.

Arthur Wellesley defeats a small force near the Danish town of Kiöge; he is named the Secretary for Ireland in the government of the Duke of Portland.

1808
Arthur Wellesley is promoted to lieutenant-general and defeats the French at Vimeiro in Portugal; his defeat of the French at Talavera in Spain earns him the title Viscount Wellington of Talavera.

1809
Napoleon's quarrel with the Pope reaches a climax when the French emperor annexes the States of the Church.

fer to Portugal where the real action is; Craig cannot spare Brock, who returns to York.

Preferring the battlefield to the council room, Wellesley returns to Portugal as commander of a British army; the ladies of Coimbra greet him enthusiastically.

1810
American troops take control of Baton Rouge from the Spanish.

Napoleon divorces Joséphine and marries Archduchess Marie Louise of Austria.

1811
Craig retires; before he leaves, he gives Brock his favourite horse, Alfred; Brock is promoted to major-general commanding British forces in Upper Canada; in October he is appointed president and provisional administrator of the government of Upper Canada with headquarters at York.

The Duke of York approves Brock's long sought-after transfer from North America.

1811
Shawnee war chief Tecumseh establishes a confederacy of Indian nations and is defeated in a battle at Tippecanoe.

Sir George Prevost, a New York-born son of Swiss parents, becomes governor general and commander-in-chief of British North America; his mother tongue is French.

Napoleon and Marie Louise have a son who is given the title King of Rome.

Britain's King George III having become permanently insane, his son, Prince George, becomes Regent.

1812
Aware that problems with the Americans may soon lead to hostilities in North America, Brock turns down a command in Spain.

1812
President Madison and the U.S. Congress declare war against Britain on June 18 and America attacks Canada as Britain's only North American possession.

BROCK AND HIS TIMES

The British and Canadians are outnumbered by the Americans, but Brock has made sure his forces are better prepared; on June 25, in an act of civilized behavior that becomes legendary, Brock crosses Lake Ontario in a bateau to Fort George, where he meets a party of Americans and sends them back to New York State under a flag of truce.

Brock's servant, Dobson, dies of an illness.

On July 16, American Fort Michilimackinac (between Lakes Huron and Michigan) falls without bloodshed to British and Canadian troops.

Brock meets Tecumseh at Amherstburg; on August 16, Brock crosses the Detroit River with 730 soldiers and militia and 600 native warriors; 2500 American troops surrender and Brock takes Fort Detroit without "the sacrifice of a drop of British blood," thus giving the British control of Michigan Territory and the Upper Mississippi.

In September, the Americans fire on Brock's flag of truce as it is carried across the Niagara River from Fort George; Brock writes to his brother Savery and says that he is anxious for the war to end so he can join Wellington in Europe.

THE CANADAS AND THE WORLD

Determined to be the only power in Europe, Napoleon invades Russia; the Russians burn Moscow; unable to maintain the long supply lines, the French retreat from Russia.

Wellington is raised to the rank of marquis.

American privateers are numerous and active in the Halifax area.

Isaac Brock

BROCK AND HIS TIMES	THE CANADAS AND THE WORLD

On October 1, Brock learns that the Americans plan to attack along the Niagara Frontier; on October 6, Brock's forty-third birthday, the bells in London ring for the fall of Fort Detroit in August.

In London, on October 10, the Prince Regent announces Brock's knighthood.

On October 12, Brock reports the amassing of a "vast number" of American troops.

On October 13, before dawn, the New York State militia crosses the Niagara River at Queenston and gains control of the heights; Brock leads the charge to regain the position and is killed by an American sharpshooter; on the same day, Brock's brothers receive his letter written in August telling them of his victory at Fort Detroit.

Major-General Sheaffe arrives with reinforcements, attacks the Americans from the rear and wins the battle; the victory raises morale and convinces Canadians that they can resist the U.S.

1813
Americans capture York briefly and burn public buildings, but neither side is able to totally control Lake Ontario; the Niagara Peninsula is a no-man's-land; American forces become so depleted that they leave Upper Canada, and burn the town

1813
Wellington leads British forces that defeat Napoleon in Spain and prepares to invade France from the south.

BROCK AND HIS TIMES

of Newark as they leave; the British burn Buffalo, New York in retaliation; Tecumseh's death at the Battle of Moraviantown marks the end of Indian resistance south of the Great Lakes.

1814

A series of battles exhausts both the Americans and the British, who burn Washington, D.C. in August; both sides capture and lose territory.

The war ends with the signing of the Treaty of Ghent on December 14; all captured territory is returned; disputed boundaries are later decided peacefully by joint border commissions.

1815

Due to the slow communications of the day, the Battle of New Orleans, a major American victory, takes place two weeks after the treaty ending the War of 1812 is signed.

THE CANADAS AND THE WORLD

1814

Wellington crosses the Pyrenees and wins the southwest of France; he is made the first Duke of Wellington; the allied forces of Europe defeat Napoleon and send him into exile on the island of Elba near Corsica.

Privateering from ports in British North America ceases with the Treaty of Ghent.

1815

Napoleon returns from exile and rules for 100 days; Wellington assumes command of the Allies' armies and defeats Napoleon at Waterloo; Napoleon is sent to St. Helena, an island off the coast of Africa.

John Franklin (future arctic explorer) is at the Battle of New Orleans with the Royal Navy.

1816

William Dummer Powell becomes Chief Justice of Upper Canada.

BROCK AND HIS TIMES

THE CANADAS AND THE WORLD

1819
Wellington becomes a member of the British cabinet.

John Franklin begins a voyage to map North America's arctic seaboard.

1820
King George III finally dies and is succeeded by his son, George IV.

1821
General Napoleon Bonaparte dies on St. Helena.

1824
Brock's body is moved from Fort George to the summit of Queenston Heights; his grave is marked by a magnificent monument.

1825
John Franklin embarks on a second voyage to chart the arctic coast from the Mackenzie River west to Prudhoe Bay.

Robert Dunsmuir (future coal magnate) is born in Scotland.

c.1826
Irving Brock (Brock's youngest brother) publishes a retranslation of François Bernier's *Travels in the Mogul Empire*.

1827
Wellington is made commander-in-chief of the British army.

BROCK AND HIS TIMES	THE CANADAS AND THE WORLD

THE CANADAS AND THE WORLD

1828
Wellington becomes prime minister of Britain but he makes many political mistakes and is not popular.

John Franklin is knighted.

1834
York, by now a fast-growing town of over 9000, is incorporated as the city of Toronto; William Lyon Mackenzie is its first mayor.

1837
Rebellions in Upper and Lower Canada.

1840
Brock's monument is destroyed.

1845
Ferdinand Brock Tupper's memoir of his uncle, Isaac, is published.

1845
Sir John Franklin leaves England on a voyage to discover the Northwest Passage.

1847
An expanded second edition of Ferdinand Brock Tupper's memoir is published.

1847
Having probably discovered the Northwest Passage, Sir John Franklin dies in his icebound ship

1851
Robert Dunsmuir arrives on Vancouver Island to mine coal for the Hudson's Bay Company.

1852
Wellington dies having possessed the obedience of the ordinary soldier, but never his love and devotion.

Isaac Brock

BROCK AND HIS TIMES	THE CANADAS AND THE WORLD

1853-56
A new monument to Brock is raised on Queenston Heights.

1865
Four-year-long American Civil War ends.

1867
The Dominion of Canada is born on July 1.

Acknowledgments
and Sources Consulted

Three people and one organization helped me write this book. Rhonda Bailey, the editorial director of XYZ Publishing, humoured me through false starts and detours. Dave Margoshes, a fellow contributor to The Quest Library, reminded me of the realm of possibility in creative nonfiction. My wife, Shelley Sopher, welcomed uninvited guests to our dinner table – guests with names like Isaac, Susan, and Elizabeth. Finally, I did much work on this project with financial support from the George Woodcock Fund, administered by The Writers' Trust of Canada.

As for sources, I depended largely on two earlier books: *The Life and Correspondence of Major-General Sir Isaac Brock, K.B.* (London: Simpkin, Marshall & Co., 2nd edition, 1847) by Ferdinand Brock Tupper; and *General Brock*, number 9 in the series The Makers of Canada (Toronto: Morang & Co., 1909) by Lady Edgar, earlier known as Matilda Ridout. What follows is a list of other books I found most useful while trying to recreate the life and times of Isaac Brock. Any errors are, of course, my own.

FITZGIBBON, Mary Agnes. *A Veteran of 1812: The Life of James FitzGibbon.* 1894. Toronto: William Briggs, 1970.

HATTERSLEY, Roy. *Nelson.* New York: Saturday Review Press, 1974.

HAYTHORNTHWAITE, Philip J. *British Infantry of the Napoleonic Wars.* London: Arms and Armour Press, 1987.

HIBBERT, Christopher. *Nelson: A Personal History.* Toronto: Viking-Penguin, 1994.

JAMES, Lawrence. *The Iron Duke: A Military Biography of Wellington.* London: Weidenfeld and Nicolson, 1992.

MALCOMSON, Robert. *The Battle of Queenston Heights.* Niagara-on-the-Lake: Friends of Fort George, 1994.

————. *Burying General Brock: A History of Brock's Monuments.* Niagara-on-the-Lake: Friends of Fort George, 1996.

MARCUS, G.J. *The Age of Nelson: The Royal Navy, 1793-1815.* New York: Viking, 1971.

MARRIN, Albert. *Napoleon and the Napoleonic Wars.* New York: Viking-Penguin, 1991.

NURSEY, Walter R. *The Story of Isaac Brock: Hero, Defender and Saviour of Upper Canada, 1812.* 1908. Toronto: William Briggs, 1909.

RACHLIS, Eugene. *The Low Countries.* Life World Library. New York: Time Inc., 1963.

ROGOZINSKI, Jan. *A Brief History of the Caribbean: From the Arawak and the Carib to the Present.* New York: Facts on File, 1992.

STANLEY, George F.G. *The War of 1812: Land*

Operations. Toronto and Ottawa: Macmillan of Canada and National Museums of Canada, 1983.

TREE, Ronald. *A History of Barbados*. London: Rupert Hart-Davis Ltd., 1972.

TURNER, Wesley B. *British Generals in the War of 1812: High Command in the Canadas*. Montreal and Kingston: McGill-Queen's University Press, 1999.

————. *The War of 1812: The War that Both Sides Won*. Toronto: Dundurn Press, 1990.

UTTLEY, John. *A Short History of the Channel Islands*. New York: Frederick A. Praeger, 1966.

WALDER, David. *Nelson*. New York: The Dial Press/James Wade, 1978.

WHIPPLE, A.B.C. et al. *Fighting Sail*. The Seafarers. Alexandra, VA: Time-Life Books, 1978.

Index

Page numbers in *italics* refer to illustrations.

Printed in September 2000
at Imprimerie Gauvin,
Hull (Québec).